THE TRIUMPH TROPHY BIBLE

Including unit-construction Trophy-based TIGER models

Also from Veloce Publishing –

Speedpro Series
4-Cylinder Engine Short Block High-Performance Manual – New Updated & Revised Edition (Hammill)
Alfa Romeo DOHC High-performance Manual (Kartalamakis)
Alfa Romeo V6 Engine High-performance Manual (Kartalamakis)
BMC 998cc A-series Engine, How to Power Tune (Hammill)
1275cc A-series High-performance Manual (Hammill)
Camshafts – How to Choose & Time Them For Maximum Power (Hammill)
Competition Car Datalogging Manual, The (Templeman)
Cylinder Heads, How to Build, Modify & Power Tune – Updated & Revised Edition (Burgess & Gollan)
Distributor-type Ignition Systems, How to Build & Power Tune – New 3rd Edition (Hammill)
Fast Road Car, How to Plan and Build – Revised & Updated Colour New Edition (Stapleton)
Ford SOHC 'Pinto' & Sierra Cosworth DOHC Engines, How to Power Tune – Updated & Enlarged Edition (Hammill)
Ford V8, How to Power Tune Small Block Engines (Hammill)
Holley Carburetors, How to Build & Power Tune – Revised & Updated Edition (Hammill)
Honda Civic Type R High-Performance Manual, The (Cowland & Clifford)
Jaguar XK Engines, How to Power Tune – Revised & Updated Colour Edition (Hammill)
Land Rover Discovery, Defender & Range Rover – How to Modify Coil Sprung Models for High Performance & Off-Road Action (Hosier)
MG Midget & Austin-Healey Sprite, How to Power Tune – New 3rd Edition (Stapleton)
MGB 4-cylinder Engine, How to Power Tune (Burgess)
MGB V8 Power, How to Give Your – Third Colour Edition (Williams)
MGB, MGC & MGB V8, How to Improve – New 2nd Edition (Williams)
Mini Engines, How to Power Tune On a Small Budget – Colour Edition (Hammill)
Motorsport, Getting Started in (Collins)
Nissan GT-R High-performance Manual, The (Gorodji)
Nitrous Oxide High-performance Manual, The (Langfield)
Race & Trackday Driving Techniques (Hornsey)
Retro or classic car for high performance, How to modify your (Stapleton)
Rover V8 Engines, How to Power Tune (Hammill)
Secrets of Speed – Today's techniques for 4-stroke engine blueprinting & tuning (Swager)
Sportscar & Kitcar Suspension & Brakes, How to Build & Modify – Revised 3rd Edition (Hammill)
SU Carburettor High-performance Manual (Hammill)
Successful Low-Cost Rally Car, How to Build a (Young)
Suzuki 4x4, How to Modify For Serious Off-road Action (Richardson)
Tiger Avon Sportscar, How to Build Your Own – Updated & Revised 2nd Edition (Dudley)
TR2, 3 & TR4, How to Improve (Williams)
TR5, 250 & TR6, How to Improve (Williams)
TR7 & TR8, How to Improve (Williams)
V8 Engine, How to Build a Short Block For High Performance (Hammill)
Volkswagen Beetle Suspension, Brakes & Chassis, How to Modify For High Performance (Hale)
Volkswagen Bus Suspension, Brakes & Chassis for High Performance, How to Modify – Updated & Enlarged New Edition (Hale)
Weber DCOE, & Dellorto DHLA Carburetors, How to Build & Power Tune – 3rd Edition (Hammill)

Enthusiast's Restoration Manual Series
Classic Large Frame Vespa Scooters, How to Restore (Paxton)
Classic Car Bodywork, How to Restore (Thaddeus)
Classic British Car Electrical Systems (Astley)
Classic Car Electrics (Thaddeus)
Jaguar E-type (Crespin)
Reliant Regal, How to Restore (Payne)
Triumph TR2, 3, 3A, 4 & 4A, How to Restore (Williams)
Triumph TR5/250 & 6, How to Restore (Williams)
Triumph TR7/8, How to Restore (Williams)
Ultimate Mini Restoration Manual, The (Ayre & Webber)
Volkswagen Beetle, How to Restore (Tyler)
VW Bay Window Bus (Paxton)

Expert Guides
Land Rover Series I-III – Your expert guide to common problems & how to fix them (Thurman)
MG Midget & A-H Sprite – Your expert guide to common problems & how to fix them (Horler)

Essential Buyer's Guide Series
Alfa Romeo Giulia GT Coupé (Booker)
Alfa Romeo Giulia Spider (Booker)
Audi TT (Davies)
Austin Seven (Barker)
Big Healeys (Trummel)
BMW E21 3 Series (1975-1983) (Cook & Reverente)
BMW E30 3 Series (1981 to 1994) (Hosier)
BMW GS (Henshaw)
BMW X5 (Saunders)
Citroën 2CV (Paxton)
Citroën ID & DS (Heilig)
Cobra Replicas (Ayre)
Corvette C2 Sting Ray 1963-1967 (Falconer)
Choosing, Using & Maintaining Your Electric Bicycle (Henshaw)
Fiat 500 & 600 (Bobbitt)
Ford Capri (Paxton)
Ford Escort Mk1 & Mk2 (Williamson)
Ford Mustang – First Generation 1964 to 1973 (Cook)
Ford Mustang – Fifth generation/S197 (Cook)
Ford RS Cosworth Sierra & Escort (Williamson)
Harley-Davidson Big Twins (Henshaw)
Hinckley Triumph triples & fours 750, 900, 955, 1000, 1050, 1200 – 1991-2009 (Henshaw)
Honda CBR FireBlade (Henshaw)
Honda CBR600 Hurricane (Henshaw)
Honda SOHC Fours 1969-1984 (Henshaw)
Jaguar E-Type 3.8 & 4.2-litre (Crespin)
Jaguar E-type V12 5.3-litre (Crespin)
Jaguar Mark 1 & 2 (All models including Daimler 2.5-litre V8) 1955 to 1969 (Thorley)
Jaguar S-Type – 1999 to 2007 (Thorley)
Jaguar X-Type – 2001 to 2009 (Thorley)
Jaguar XJ-S (Crespin)
Jaguar XJ6, XJ8 & XJR (Thorley)
Jaguar XK 120, 140 & 150 (Thorley)
Jaguar XK8 & XKR (1996-2005) (Thorley)
Jaguar/Daimler XJ 1994-2003 (Crespin)
Jaguar/Daimler XJ40 (Crespin)
Jaguar/Daimler XJ6, XJ12 & Sovereign (Crespin)
Kawasaki Z1 & Z900 (Orritt)
Land Rover Series I, II & IIA (Thurman)
Land Rover Series III (Thurman)
Lotus Seven replicas & Caterham 7: 1973-2013 (Hawkins)
Mazda MX-5 Miata (Mk1 1989-97 & Mk2 98-2001) (Crook)
Mazda RX-8 All models 2003 to 2012 (Parish)
Mercedes Benz Pagoda 230SL, 250SL & 280SL roadsters & coupés (Bass)
Mercedes-Benz 280-560SL & SLC (Bass)
Mercedes-Benz SL R129 Series (Parish)
Mercedes-Benz W124 – All models 1984-1997 (Zoporowski)
MG Midget & A-H Sprite (Horler)
MG TD, TF & TF1500 (Jones)
MGA 1955-1962 (Crosier)
MGB & MGB GT (Williams)
MGF & MG TF (Hawkins)
Mini (Paxton)
Morris Minor & 1000 (Newell)
Moto Guzzi 2-valve big twins (Falloon)
New Mini (Collins)
Norton Commando (Henshaw)
Peugeot 205 GTI (Blackburn)
Porsche 911 (964) (Streather)
Porsche 911 (993) (Streather)
Porsche 911 (996) (Streather)
Porsche 911 (997) Model years 2004 to 2009 (Streather)
Porsche 911 (997) Second generation models 2009 to 2012 (Streather)
Porsche 911 Carrera 3.2 (Streather)
Porsche 911 SC (Streather)
Porsche 924 – All models 1976 to 1988 (Hodgkins)
Porsche 928 (Hemmings)
Porsche 930 Turbo & 911 (930) Turbo (Streather)
Porsche 944 (Higgins)
Porsche 986 Boxster (Streather)
Porsche 987 Boxster & Cayman (Streather)
Rolls-Royce Silver Shadow & Bentley T-Series (Bobbitt)
Royal Enfield Bullet (Henshaw)
Subaru Impreza (Hobbs)
Sunbeam Alpine (Barker)
Triumph 350 & 500 Twins (Henshaw)
Triumph Bonneville (Henshaw)
Triumph Herald & Vitesse (Davies)
Triumph Spitfire & GT6 (Baugues)
Triumph Stag (Mort)
Triumph Thunderbird, Trophy & Tiger (Henshaw)
Triumph TR6 (Williams)
Triumph TR7 & TR8 (Williams)
Velocette 350 & 500 Singles (Henshaw)
Vespa Scooters – Classic 2-stroke models 1960-2008 (Paxton)
Volvo 700/900 Series (Beavis)
VW Beetle (Cservenka & Copping)
VW Bus (Cservenka & Copping)
VW Golf GTI (Cservenka & Copping)

Those Were The Days ... Series
Alpine Trials & Rallies 1910-1973 (Pfundner)
American 'Independent' Automakers – AMC to Willys 1945 to 1960 (Mort)
American Station Wagons – The Golden Era 1950-1975 (Mort)
American Trucks of the 1950s (Mort)
American Trucks of the 1960s (Mort)
American Woodies 1928-1953 (Mort)
Anglo-American Cars from the 1930s to the 1970s (Mort)
Austerity Motoring (Bobbitt)
Austins, The last real (Peck)
Brighton National Speed Trials (Gardiner)
British and European Trucks of the 1970s (Peck)
British Drag Racing – The early years (Pettitt)
British Lorries of the 1950s (Bobbitt)
British Lorries of the 1960s (Bobbitt)
British Touring Car Racing (Collins)
British Police Cars (Walker)
British Woodies (Peck)
Café Racer Phenomenon, The (Walker)
Don Hayter's MGB Story – The birth of the MGB in MG's Abingdon Design & Development Office (Hayter)
Drag Bike Racing in Britain – From the mid '60s to the mid '80s (Lee)
Dune Buggy Phenomenon, The (Hale)
Dune Buggy Phenomenon Volume 2, The (Hale)
Endurance Racing at Silverstone in the 1970s & 1980s (Parker)
Hot Rod & Stock Car Racing in Britain in the 1980s (Neil)
Last Real Austins 1946-1959, The (Peck)
Mercedes-Benz Trucks (Peck)
MG's Abingdon Factory (Moylan)
Motor Racing at Brands Hatch in the Seventies (Parker)
Motor Racing at Brands Hatch in the Eighties (Parker)
Motor Racing at Crystal Palace (Collins)
Motor Racing at Goodwood in the Sixties (Gardiner)
Motor Racing at Nassau in the 1950s & 1960s (O'Neil)
Motor Racing at Oulton Park in the 1960s (McFadyen)
Motor Racing at Oulton Park in the 1970s (McFadyen)
Motor Racing at Thruxton in the 1970s (Grant-Braham)
Motor Racing at Thruxton in the 1980s (Grant-Braham)
Superprix – The Story of Birmingham Motor Race (Page & Collins)
Three Wheelers (Bobbitt)

Rally Giants Series
Audi Quattro (Robson)
Austin Healey 100-6 & 3000 (Robson)
Fiat 131 Abarth (Robson)
Ford Escort MkI (Robson)
Ford Escort RS Cosworth & World Rally Car (Robson)
Ford Escort RS1800 (Robson)
Lancia Delta 4WD/Integrale (Robson)
Lancia Stratos (Robson)
Mini Cooper/Mini Cooper S (Robson)
Peugeot 205 T16 (Robson)
Saab 96 & V4 (Robson)
Subaru Impreza (Robson)
Toyota Celica GT4 (Robson)

WSC Giants
Audi R8 (Wagstaff)
Ferrari 312P & 312PB (Collins & McDonough)
Gulf-Mirage 1967 to 1982 (McDonough)
Matra Sports Cars – MS620, 630, 650, 660 & 670 – 1966 to 1974 (McDonough)

General
11/2-litre GP Racing 1961-1965 (Whitelock)
AC Two-litre Saloons & Buckland Sportscars (Archibald)
Alfa Romeo 155/156/147 Competition Touring Cars (Collins)
Alfa Romeo Giulia Coupé GT & GTA (Tipler)
Alfa Romeo Montreal – The dream car that came true (Taylor)
Alfa Romeo Montreal – The Essential Companion (Classic Reprint of 500 copies) (Taylor)
Alfa Tipo 33 (McDonough & Collins)
Alpine & Renault – The Development of the Revolutionary Turbo F1 Car 1968 to 1979 (Smith)
Alpine & Renault – The Sports Prototypes 1963 to 1969 (Smith)
Alpine & Renault – The Sports Prototypes 1973 to 1978 (Smith)
Anatomy of the Classic Mini (Huthert & Ely)
Anatomy of the Works Minis (Moylan)
Armstrong-Siddeley (Smith)
Art Deco and British Car Design (Down)
Autodrome (Collins & Ireland)
Autodrome 2 (Collins & Ireland)
Automotive A-Z, Lane's Dictionary of Automotive Terms (Lane)
Automotive Mascots (Kay & Springate)
Bahamas Speed Weeks, The (O'Neil)
Bentley Continental, Corniche and Azure (Bennett)
Bentley MkVI, Rolls-Royce Silver Wraith, Dawn & Cloud/Bentley R & S-Series (Nutland)
Bluebird CN7 (Stevens)
BMC Competitions Department Secrets (Turner, Chambers & Browning)
BMW 5-Series (Cranswick)
BMW Z-Cars (Taylor)
BMW Boxer Twins 1970-1995 Bible, The (Falloon)
BMW Cafe Racers (Cloesen)
BMW Custom Motorcycles – Choppers, Cruisers, Bobbers, Trikes & Quads (Cloesen)
BMW – The Power of M (Vivian)
Bonjour – Is this Italy? (Turner)
British 250cc Racing Motorcycles (Pereira)
British at Indianapolis, The (Wagstaff)
British Café Racers (Cloesen)
British Cars, The Complete Catalogue of, 1895-1975 (Culshaw & Horrobin)
British Custom Motorcycles – The Brit Chop – choppers, cruisers, bobbers & trikes (Cloesen)
BRM – A Mechanic's Tale (Salmon)
BRM V16 (Ludvigsen)
BSA Bantam Bible, The (Henshaw)
BSA Motorcycles – the final evolution (Jones)
Bugatti Type 40 (Price)
Bugatti 46/50 Updated Edition (Price & Arbey)
Bugatti T44 & T49 (Price & Arbey)
Bugatti 57 2nd Edition (Price)
Bugatti Type 57 Grand Prix – A Celebration (Tomlinson)
Caravan, Improve & Modify Your (Porter)
Caravans, The Illustrated History 1919-1959 (Jenkinson)
Caravans, The Illustrated History From 1960 (Jenkinson)
Carrera Panamericana, La (Tipler)
Chrysler 300 – America's Most Powerful Car 2nd Edition (Ackerson)
Chrysler PT Cruiser (Ackerson)
Citroën DS (Bobbitt)
Classic British Car Electrical Systems (Astley)
Cobra – The Real Thing! (Legate)
Competition Car Aerodynamics 3rd Edition (McBeath)
Competition Car Composites A Practical Handbook (Revised 2nd Edition) (McBeath)
Concept Cars, How to illustrate and design (Dewey)
Cortina – Ford's Bestseller (Robson)
Coventry Climax Racing Engines (Hammill)
Daily Mirror 1970 World Cup Rally 40, The (Robson)
Daimler SP250 New Edition (Long)
Datsun Fairlady Roadster to 280ZX – The Z-Car Story (Long)
Dino – The V6 Ferrari (Long)
Dodge Challenger & Plymouth Barracuda (Grist)
Dodge Charger – Enduring Thunder (Ackerson)
Dodge Dynamite! (Grist)
Dorset from the Sea – The Jurassic Coast from Lyme Regis to Old Harry Rocks photographed from its best viewpoint (Belasco)
Dorset from the Sea – The Jurassic Coast from Lyme Regis to Old Harry Rocks photographed from its best viewpoint (souvenir edition) (Belasco)
Draw & Paint Cars – How to (Gardiner)
Drive on the Wild Side, A – 20 Extreme Driving Adventures From Around the World (Weaver)
Ducati 750 Bible, The (Falloon)
Ducati 750 SS 'round-case' 1974, The Book of the (Falloon)
Ducati 860, 900 and Mille Bible, The (Falloon)
Ducati Monster Bible (New Updated & Revised Edition), The (Falloon)
Ducati 916 (updated edition) (Falloon)
Dune Buggy, Building A – The Essential Manual (Shakespeare)
Dune Buggy Files (Hale)
Dune Buggy Handbook (Hale)
East German Motor Vehicles in Pictures (Suhr/Weinreich)
Fast Ladies – Female Racing Drivers 1888 to 1970 (Bouzanquet)
Fate of the Sleeping Beauties, The (op de Weegh/Hottendorff/op de Weegh)
Ferrari 288 GTO, The Book of the (Sackey)
Ferrari 333 SP (O'Neil)
Fiat & Abarth 124 Spider & Coupé (Tipler)
Fiat & Abarth 500 & 600 – 2nd Edition (Bobbitt)
Fiats, Great Small (Ward)
Fine Art of the Motorcycle Engine, The (Peirce)
Ford Cleveland 335-Series V8 engine 1970 to 1982 – The Essential Source Book (Hammill)
Ford F100/F150 Pick-up 1948-1996 (Ackerson)
Ford F150 Pick-up 1997-2005 (Ackerson)
Ford GT – Then, and Now (Streather)
Ford GT40 (Legate)
Ford Midsize Muscle – Fairlane, Torino & Ranchero (Cranswick)
Ford Model Y (Roberts)
Ford Small Block V8 Racing Engines 1962-1970 – The Essential Source Book (Hammill)
Ford Thunderbird From 1954, The Book of the (Long)
Formula 5000 Motor Racing, Back then ... and back now (Lawson)
Forza Minardi! (Vigar)
France: the essential guide for car enthusiasts – 200 things for the car enthusiast to see and do (Parish)
From Crystal Palace to Red Square – A Hapless Biker's Road to Russia (Turner)
Funky Mopeds (Skelton)
Grand Prix Ferrari – The Years of Enzo Ferrari's Power, 1948-1980 (Pritchard)
Grand Prix Ford – DFV-powered Formula 1 Cars (Robson)
GT – The World's Best GT Cars 1953-73 (Dawson)
Hillclimbing & Sprinting – The Essential Manual (Short & Wilkinson)
Honda NSX (Long)
Inside the Rolls-Royce & Bentley Styling Department – 1971 to 2001 (Hull)
Intermeccanica – The Story of the Prancing Bull (McCredie & Reisner)
Italian Cafe Racers (Cloesen)
Italian Custom Motorcycles (Cloesen)
Jaguar, The Rise of (Price)
Jaguar XJ 220 – The Inside Story (Moreton)
Jaguar XJ-S, The Book of the (Long)
Jeep CJ (Ackerson)
Jeep Wrangler (Ackerson)
The Jowett Jupiter – The car that leaped to fame (Nankivell)
Karmann-Ghia Coupé & Convertible (Bobbitt)
Kawasaki Triples Bible, The (Walker)
Kawasaki Z1 Story, The (Sheehan)
Kris Meeke – Intercontinental Rally Challenge Champion (McBride)
Lamborghini Miura Bible, The (Sackey)
Lamborghini Urraco, The Book of the (Landsem)
Lambretta Bible, The (Davies)
Lancia 037 (Collins)
Lancia Delta HF Integrale (Blaettel & Wagner)
Land Rover Series III Reborn (Porter)
Land Rover, The Half-ton Military (Cook)
Laverda Twins & Triples Bible 1968-1986 (Falloon)
Lea-Francis Story, The (Price)
Le Mans Panoramic (Ireland)
Lexus Story, The (Long)
Lola – The Illustrated History (1957-1977) (Starkey)
Lola – All the Sports Racing & Single-seater Racing Cars 1978-1997 (Starkey)
Lola T70 – The Racing History & Individual Chassis Record – 4th Edition (Starkey)
Lotus 18 Colin Chapman's U-turn (Whitelock)
Lotus 49 (Oliver)
Marketingmobiles, The Wonderful Wacky World of (Hale)
Maserati 250F In Focus (Pritchard)
Mazda MX-5/Miata 1.6 Enthusiast's Workshop Manual (Grainger & Shoemark)
Mazda MX-5/Miata 1.8 Enthusiast's Workshop Manual (Grainger & Shoemark)
Mazda MX-5 Miata, The book of the – The 'Mk1' NA-series 1988 to 1997 (Long)
Mazda MX-5 Miata Roadster (Long)
Mazda Rotary-engined Cars (Cranshaw)
Maximum Mini (Booij)
Meet the English (Bowie)
Mercedes-Benz SL – R230 series 2001 to 2011 (Long)
Mercedes-Benz SL – W113-series 1963-1971 (Long)
Mercedes-Benz SL & SLC – 107-series 1971-1989 (Long)
Mercedes-Benz SLK – R170 series 1996-2004 (Long)
Mercedes-Benz SLK – R171 series 2004-2011 (Long)
Mercedes-Benz W123-series – All models 1976 to 1986 (Long)
Mercedes G-Wagen (Long)
MGA (Price Williams)
MGB & MGB GT- Expert Guide (Auto-doc Series) (Williams)
MGB Electrical Systems Updated & Revised Edition (Astley)
Microcars at Large! (Quellin)
Mini Cooper – The Real Thing! (Tipler)
Mini Minor to Asia Minor (West)
Mitsubishi Lancer Evo, The Road Car & WRC Story (Long)
Montlhéry, The Story of the Paris Autodrome (Boddy)
Morgan Maverick (Lawrence)
Morgan 3 Wheeler – back to the future!, The (Dron)
Morris Minor, 60 Years on the Road (Newell)
Moto Guzzi Sport & Le Mans Bible, The (Falloon)
Motor Movies – The Posters! (Veysey)
Motor Racing – Reflections of a Lost Era (Carter)
Motor Racing – The Pursuit of Victory 1930-1962 (Carter)
Motor Racing – The Pursuit of Victory 1963-1972 (Wyatt/Sears)
Motor Racing Heroes – The Stories of 100 Greats (Newman)
Motorhomes, The Illustrated History (Jenkinson)
Motorsport In colour, 1950s (Wainwright)
MV Agusta Fours, The book of the classic (Falloon)
N.A.R.T. – A concise history of the North American Racing Team 1957 to 1983 (O'Neil)
Nissan 300ZX & 350Z – The Z-Car Story (Long)
Nissan GT-R Supercar: Born to race (Gorodji)
Northeast American Sports Car Races 1950-1959 (O'Neil)
Nothing Runs – Misadventures in the Classic, Collectable & Exotic Car Biz (Slutsky)
Peking to Paris 2007 (Young)
Pontiac Firebird (Cranswick)
Porsche Boxster (Long)
Porsche 356 (2nd Edition) (Long)
Porsche 908 (Födisch, Neßhöver, Roßbach, Schwarz & Roßbach)
Porsche 911 Carrera – The Last of the Evolution (Corlett)
Porsche 911R, RS & RSR, 4th Edition (Starkey)
Porsche 911, The Book of the (Long)
Porsche – The Racing 914s (Smith)
Porsche 911SC 'Super Carrera' – The Essential Companion (Streather)
Porsche 914 & 914-6: The Definitive History of the Road & Competition Cars (Long)
Porsche 924 (Long)
The Porsche 924 Carreras – evolution to excellence (Smith)
Porsche 928 (Long)
Porsche 944 (Long)
Porsche 964, 993 & 996 Data Plate Code Breaker (Streather)
Porsche 993 'King Of Porsche' – The Essential Companion (Streather)
Porsche 996 'Supreme Porsche' – The Essential Companion (Streather)
Porsche 997 2004-2012 – Porsche Excellence (Streather)
Porsche Racing Cars – 1953 to 1975 (Long)
Porsche Racing Cars – 1976 to 2005 (Long)
Porsche – The Rally Story (Meredith)
Porsche: Three Generations of Genius (Meredith)
Preston Tucker & Others (Linde)
RAC Rally Action! (Gardiner)
RACING COLOURS – MOTOR RACING COMPOSITIONS 1908-2009 (Newman)
Rallye Sport Fords: The Inside Story (Moreton)
Roads with a View – England's greatest views and how to find them by road (Corfield)
Rolls-Royce Silver Shadow/Bentley T Series Corniche & Camargue – Revised & Enlarged Edition (Bobbitt)
Rolls-Royce Silver Spirit, Silver Spur & Bentley Mulsanne 2nd Edition (Bobbitt)
Rover P4 (Bobbitt)
Runways & Racers (O'Neil)
Russian Motor Vehicles – Soviet Limousines 1930-2003 (Kelly)
Russian Motor Vehicles – The Czarist Period 1784 to 1917 (Kelly)
RX-7 – Mazda's Rotary Engine Sportscar (Updated & Revised New Edition) (Long)
Singer Story: Cars, Commercial Vehicles, Bicycles & Motorcycle (Atkinson)
Sleeping Beauties USA – abandoned classic cars & trucks (Marek)
SM – Citroën's Maserati-engined Supercar (Long & Claverol)
Speedway – Auto racing's ghost tracks (Collins & Ireland)
Sprite Caravans, The Story of (Jenkinson)
Standard Motor Company, The Book of the (Robson)
Steve Hole's Kit Car Cornucopia – Cars, Companies, Stories, Facts & Figures: the UK's kit car scene since 1949 (Hole)
Subaru Impreza: The Road Car And WRC Story (Long)
Supercar, How to Build your own (Thompson)
Tales from the Toolbox (Oliver)
Tatra – The Legacy of Hans Ledwinka, Updated & Enlarged Collector's Edition of 1500 copies (Margolius & Henry)
Toleman Story, The (Hilton)
Toyota Celica & Supra, The Book of Toyota's Sports Coupés (Long)
Toyota MR2 Coupés & Spyders (Long)
Triumph Bonneville Bible (59-83) (Henshaw)
Triumph Bonneville!, Save the – The inside story of the Meriden Workers' Co-op (Rosamond)
Triumph Motorcycles & the Meriden Factory (Hancox)
Triumph Speed Twin & Thunderbird Bible (Woolridge)
Triumph Tiger Cub Bible (Estall)
Triumph Trophy Bible (Woolridge)
Two Summers – The Mercedes-Benz W196R Racing Car (Ackerson)
TWR Story, The – Group A (Hughes & Scott)
Unraced (Collins)
Velocette Motorcycles – MSS to Thruxton – New Third Edition (Burris)
Vespa – The Story of a Cult Classic in Pictures (Uhlig)
Vincent Motorcycles: The Untold Story since 1946 (Guyony & Parker)
Volkswagen Bus Book, The (Bobbitt)
Volkswagen Bus or Van to Camper, How to Convert (Porter)
Volkswagens of the World (Glen)
VW Beetle Cabriolet – The full story of the convertible Beetle (Bobbitt)
VW Beetle – The Car of the 20th Century (Copping)
VW Bus – 40 Years of Splitties, Bays & Wedges (Copping)
VW Bus Book, The (Bobbitt)
VW Golf: Five Generations of Fun (Copping & Cservenka)
VW – The Air-cooled Era (Copping)
VW T5 Camper Conversion Manual (Porter)
VW Campers (Copping)
You & Your Jaguar XK8/XKR – Buying, Enjoying, Maintaining, Modifying – New Edition (Thorley)
Which Oil? – Choosing the right oils & greases for your antique, vintage, veteran, classic or collector car (Michell)

For post publication news, updates and amendments relating to this book please visit: www.veloce.co.uk/books/V4974

www.veloce.co.uk

First published in 2002 by Veloce Publishing Limited, Veloce House, Parkway Farm Business Park, Middle Farm Way, Poundbury, Dorchester, Dorset, DT1 3AR, England.
Fax 01305 250479/e-mail info@veloce.co.uk/web www.veloce.co.uk or www.velocebooks.com.
Reprinted 2003, 2006, November 2007, August 2010.
This edition printed May 2016, reprinted October 2016. ISBN: 978-1-845849-74-0 UPC: 6-36847-04974-4
© Harry Woolridge and Veloce Publishing 2002, 2003, 2006, 2007, 2010 and 2016. All rights reserved. With the exception of quoting brief passages for the purpose of review, no part of this publication may be recorded, reproduced or transmitted by any means, including photocopying, without the written permission of Veloce Publishing Ltd. Throughout this book logos, model names and designations, etc, have been used for the purposes of identification, illustration and decoration. Such names are the property of the trademark holder as this is not an official publication.
Readers with ideas for automotive books, or books on other transport or related hobby subjects, are invited to write to the editorial director of Veloce Publishing at the above address.
British Library Cataloguing in Publication Data – A catalogue record for this book is available from the British Library. Typesetting, design and page make-up all by Veloce Publishing Ltd on Apple Mac. Printed by CPI Group (UK) Ltd, Croydon, CR04YY.

Veloce Classic Reprint Series

THE TRIUMPH TROPHY BIBLE

Including unit-construction Trophy-based TIGER models

– Harry Woolridge –

VELOCE PUBLISHING
THE PUBLISHER OF FINE AUTOMOTIVE BOOKS

Contents

Introduction 5
  Preface 5
  Acknowledgements 5
  About the author.. 5

Chapter 1 A brief history of the company 6

Chapter 2 The Triumph Trophy 9
  International Six Days Trials 26

Chapter 3 Technical development 39
  1949 TR5 Trophy 39
  1949 TR5 Trophy 42
  1950 TR5 Trophy 44
  1951 TR5 Trophy 45
  1952 TR5 Trophy 47
  1953 TR5 Trophy 48
  1954 TR5 Trophy 49
  1955 TR5 Trophy 49
  Summary of 1955 TR5 changes.......................... 51
  1956 TR5 and TR6 Trophy - Variation TR5/R... 51
  1956 TR6... 53
  1956 TR5R... 53
  1957 TR5 and TR6 Trophy 54
  1958 TR5 and TR6 Trophy 56
  1959 TR5 and TR6.. 58
  1960 TR6 Trophy TR6A and TR6B variants...... 61
  1961 TR6 Trophy TR6R and TR6C variants...... 63
  1962 TR6 S/S Trophy.. 69
  1963 TR6 S/S 69
  1964 TR6 Trophy.. 72
  1965 TR6 Trophy TR6SS, TR6SR, TR6SC,
    TR6... 73
  1966 TR6... 74
  1967 TR6 Trophy.. 79
  1968 TR6... 82
  1969 Model Tiger TR6.. 86
  1970 TR6 Tiger 87
  1971 TR6 Tiger 90
  1972 TR6 Tiger 95
  1973 TR6 and TR7 Tiger.................................... 97
  1974 TR7 Tiger 99

  1975 TR7 Tiger 100
  1976 TR7 Tiger 100
  1977 TR7 Tiger 101
  1978 TR7 Tiger 101
  1979 TR7 Tiger 102
  1980 TR7 Tiger 103
  1981 TR7 Tiger 104
  1982 TR7 Tiger 104
  1983 TR7 Tiger and TR65 106

**Chapter 4 1961 - 1974
unit construction 490cc**...................................107
  1961 TR5AC, 1962 T100SC, 1966
    T100C, 1972 TR5T year on year model
    description.. 107
  1961 TR5AR, TR5AC technical data 107
  1961 Model TR5AC Trophy..............................110
  1962 Model Trophy T100S/C 116
  1963 Model T100S/C...116
  1964 Model T100S/C...117
  1965 Model T100S/C...119
  1966 Model T100 S/C....................................... 121
  1967 Model T100C Sports Tiger...................... 122
  1968 Model T100C Sports Tiger...................... 124
  1969 Model T100C Trophy 500....................... 125
  1970 Model T100C Trophy 500....................... 127
  1971 Model T100C Trophy 500....................... 128
  1972 Model TR5T Trophy Trail........................ 130
  1973 Model TR5T Trophy Trail........................ 130
  1974 Model TR5T Trophy Trail Adventurer..... 132

Appendix 133
  Colour chart TR5, TR6, TR7 133
  Colour chart 500 unit.. 136
  Model year build totals 137
  Works registered Trophy models...................... 137
  Notable registration numbers associated
    with the Trophy model................................... 138
  Trophy show models 139
  Trophy carburettor specification 140

Index..142

Introduction

Preface

It's now over ten years since I last put pen to paper and compiled the Triumph Speed Twin book, which, I was very pleased to learn, a good many enthusiasts considered a useful guide to restoration. Over the years many asked if I had given any thought to doing the same for the Trophy. As it's always been my favourite model, I needed little persuasion and I hope those who read this book get as much enjoyment from it as I got in compiling it.

Acknowledgements

I would like to thank all those who have helped in compiling this book. I was fortunate that many of my friends were also my workmates at Triumph so the pooling of knowledge was very useful.

Special thanks to John Nelson for the use of his photographic library, and to Miss Louise Betteridge for her patience in setting out and typing the original manuscript.

About the Author

Always a keen motorcyclist, I actually began my working life at Jaguar and Singer Cars in Coventry, before getting called up for National Service in the Royal Air Force. Posted to Egypt as a vehicle fitter, my motorcycling was curtailed somewhat, since the only bikes available were Norton 16H side valves (not the ideal mount for desert riding ...).

Released from the RAF, I worked as a fitter for British Road Services, mainly on Foden, Sentinel and AEC diesel trucks. Being an enthusiastic motorcyclist, however, I soon applied for a job in the Service Department at the Triumph Engineering Company, and was lucky enough to be selected. Thus began a relationship with Triumph and its motorcycles that lasted thirty years, and, in retrospect, is one I would not have missed at any price.

After a few years in the Service Department, I joined the team in the Experimental Department where I remained for five glorious years, and was eventually promoted to the position of Assistant Quality Control Manager. Later, in a reshuffle of titles, I became Inspection Foreman for Motorcycle Assembly and Production Development.

With the formation of the Meriden Co-operative, I served as Warranty/Service Manager until closure in 1983.

Harry Woolridge
Nuneaton

Chapter 1

A brief history of the company

The origins of the Triumph motorcycle company go back to 1885, when a young German, Siegfried Bettmann, moved to London and started an import/export business selling pedal cycles branded with his own name.

In 1886, Bettmann changed the company name to Triumph, reasoning that its meaning was self explanatory, and also because it translated well into many European languages. During 1887, Bettmann was joined by Mauritz Shulte, a young German engineer. A year later they moved to Coventry and rented a small factory with the intention of manufacturing their own machines. Bettmann and Shulte reasoned that Coventry, being the centre of the cycle industry, would be an ideal manufacturing base since it was close to suppliers and boasted a plentiful supply of skilled labour.

In 1902, the company produced its first motorcycle, using a Belgian 2¼hp Minerva engine clipped to a bicycle frame. It was not long, however, before a Shulte-designed engine was built, and 1905 saw a totally in-house Triumph of 3hp (363cc) being offered for sale.

By 1915, the engine capacity had increased to 550cc, and the machine now looked like a proper motorcycle (gone were the pedals of previous years). The machine was fitted with a three speed gearbox, though a belt was still used for the final drive. This motorcycle, the Model H, was supplied to despatch riders during WWI, and soon gained a reputation for quality and reliability in the mud of the Western Front. The term 'trusty triumph' originated in this period, and the company used it when advertising the model.

Triumph had experimented with a 600cc vertical twin as early as 1913, but the 1914-18 war halted development. This was the first known vertical twin from Triumph. Later, in 1933, a Val Page-designed 633cc vertical twin was produced. Unfortunately, being rather old fashioned in appearance, it did not win public acclaim.

1935 saw the company fall into financial difficulty, like so many others during the depression of the 1930s.

So serious were the problems, in fact, that the company went into bankruptcy, and closed completely in 1936.

The pedal cycle part of the company was sold to Raleigh Cycles, Nottingham, and the motorcar side to the Standard Motor Company, Coventry. Most of the motorcycle manufacturing business was purchased by Mr Jack Sangster, then owner of Ariel Motors, Birmingham, for the reputed figure of £30,000. The factory and the plant were leased from a Mr Graham, the official receiver appointed by Lloyds Bank, and spares were sold on commission, thus reducing the original outlay.

It didn't take long for the newly formed 'Triumph Engineering Company Limited' to start production of motorcycles. This was largely because Sangster had sent one of his most competent Ariel men, Edward Turner, to Coventry to be General Manager and Chief Designer.

This appointment was to prove inspirational, and, as we now know, the company went on to become one of Britain's most successful motorcycle firms. It wasn't long before the youthful 35 year old Edward had designed a vertical twin which would change the course of motorcycle design for the next three decades. Although the vertical twin concept was copied by most of the British manufacturers, good as they were, the Triumph stayed pre-eminent.

When the first Triumph twins arrived in the USA, just prior to WWII, they were an outstanding success; taking on and beating the Indians and Harleys, which were often twice the engine capacity of the Triumph, and winning races on the speedway tracks and in hill climbs. Edward Turner, who regarded himself as chief salesman as well as designer and financial director, soon saw a potential sales outlet in the USA. To this end he had started corresponding with a Mr Bill Johnson of Pasadena, a lawyer and keen motorcyclist. This correspondence soon blossomed into a strong personal and business relationship, and, when Johnson wanted

A brief history of the company

to open a motorcycle store, the Triumph marque was a natural choice.

Having set up a successful West Coast sales outlet, Triumph now looked to the East Coast. The company engaged the services of Mr Dennis McCormack, a forty-eight year old mechanical engineer who, before becoming an American citizen, had actually been born in Coventry. McCormack took a lease on premises in Joppa Road, Towson, near Baltimore in Maryland, and set up the Triumph Corporation, subsequently known as Tri-Cor. This East Coast outlet soon began to rival Jomo in terms of sales and service.

Turner was not slow to capitalise on the US setup, and spent many months each year visiting the two distributorships.

All this seemed to point to a very rosy future for Triumph, but a certain Herr Hitler was soon going to change this. One cold November night in 1940, the Coventry factory was completely destroyed in one of the worst bombing raids the city had experienced. However, with true Coventrian grit and determination, the remains were sifted through and anything that could be of use was transported to the nearby town of Warwick. Spares were soon being produced from the tin shed that served as a factory, and, by mid 1941, complete motorcycles were being manufactured for the allied armed forces.

A completely new factory was built in 1942 just outside Coventry, near Meriden Village (allegedly the centre of England). Up until 1945, however, the factory only produced machines for the War Department (these were the 3SW and 5SW 350 and 500cc side valves, and the 3HW 350cc overhead valve).

On the cessation of hostilities, Triumph was in an enviable position. The post-war twins were in great demand and the company had a nearly new factory in which to produce them. With telescopic front forks replacing the old girder units, a spring hub at the rear wheel, and a few engine modifications, Triumphs were ready for the post-war boom.

Despite this apparently bright future, though, there were many frustrations to overcome in the immediate post-war years. Steel rationing was in force, with priority being given to exporters (luckily, though, Triumph was one of these). Petrol and raw materials like rubber were also in short supply. Even electricity was rationed, being available only on certain days of the week. Triumph's answer to this was to install its own generator.

Although motorcycles did get produced despite these problems, the demand was so great that it couldn't be satisfied, and waiting lists grew ever longer. There were even waiting lists in the 1950s and 1960s, and it was suggested that Edward Turner kept the market short intentionally, thereby boosting demand.

In 1951, Jack Sangster sold his interest in the Triumph Engineering Co. Ltd. to the Birmingham Small Arms Company (BSA), whilst Turner stayed on at Triumph as Managing Director. Although the rivalry between Triumph and BSA didn't diminish, the profits, which had previously stayed with the Triumph company and its shareholders, would in future go into the BSA group purse.

Jack Sangster and Edward Turner were on the BSA board of directors, but the Triumph company was left to run with very little BSA interference, possibly due to the fact that profits at Meriden were so good.

During May 1961, Bert Hopwood rejoined the Triumph company as Director and General Manager. Jack Sangster resigned as Chairman of BSA, and Mr Eric Turner (no relation to Edward) was appointed in his place.

In 1964, Edward Turner announced his retirement as Divisional Executive Director, but retained a seat on the BSA group board in a non-executive capacity. By mid-1964, Mr Harry Sturgeon had been appointed Chief Executive of the BSA Motorcycle Division, and Bert Hopwood gained the title of Engineering Director and Deputy Director of the Division. Unfortunately, Harry Sturgeon took ill and died of a brain tumour in 1966. His short time as Chief Executive, however, had seen the motorcycle group's turnover increase by nearly 40%. This was a welcome rise in production, since all the group's models had been in great demand, especially in the USA.

One might have assumed that, as Deputy Director, Bert Hopwood would have been promoted, but this was not the case. Instead, a Mr Lionel Jofeh was appointed by Eric Turner, and given the title of Managing Director of the group's Automotive Division, the inept management of which hastened the eventual downfall of the group. For some reason Jofeh took a great dislike to the Triumph setup, and detested any successes achieved by the company, even threatening to dismiss anyone who was seen to be favouring Triumph over BSA!

Jofeh soon established a group engineering centre at Umberslade Hall, an old country mansion near Hockley Heath, midway between the Triumph and BSA factories. Mr Mike Needham, who came from the aircraft industry, took up the post of Deputy Engineering Director and undertook to set up Umberslade. He collected the design and development staff, which would ultimately number over 300, from the three existing factories. A couple of men were left in the design department at Triumph to cover day to day anomalies, and to liaise with Umberslade should the need arise.

It seemed that all was not going well with the motorcycle group, as high level jobs with fancy titles (and attendant high salaries) were being created almost daily. Departments, which had previously been housed in one factory, were split up, and duplication of functions was commonplace. The latter became apparent when the engineering meetings, which had previously taken place in ordinary-sized offices, had become so well attended that BSA found difficulty finding locations large enough to accommodate everyone.

'Critical path analysis' and 'production evaluation' were the 'in things' at Triumph. Even though they did little to aid production, the motions still had to be adhered to. This caused much frustration and ill feeling amongst the workforce.

The Research and Development department at Umberslade Hall was becoming a luxury that the motorcycle division couldn't afford. It certainly seemed to the folk at Meriden that there was a lot of input to the department, in terms of staff and resources, but there was little to show for it (unless one took into account the increase in the number of peacocks around the grounds).

For the 1971 season, the Triumph factory was supposed to be building a new 650cc motorcycle designed by the Research and Development department at Umberslade Hall. The production build dates came and went, with the factory yet to see any drawings, so no jigs and fixtures could be produced which would have enabled production to commence. Eventually, the new 650 reached Triumph some three months late. Unfortunately, however, it was found that an assembled engine unit could not be fitted into the frame. Numerous modifications were made by the Meriden design staff, much to the chagrin of the Umberslade team. Another design error concerned the height of the seat on the completed machine. At 34 inches from ground level it was just too high for most people. Triumph complained at this, only to be told by Umberslade that the frames had not been made correctly, as per the drawings, so it was Triumph's problem. To counter this accusation, Triumph had the frames independently inspected and, although the report did indeed show that the frames were taller than the drawings specified, it was only by one thirty second of an inch ($1/32$in). Triumph was completely vindicated.

By now, as one can imagine, feelings between Meriden and Umberslade were getting quite bitter, and various derogatory names were found for the mansion (Slumberglades was the favourite).

In July 1971, due to the financial state of the group, Jofeh agreed to resign his post as Managing Director and his contract was bought out. A new Chief Executive, Mr Brian Eustace, was appointed in November, replacing Eric Turner who stayed on in an advisory capacity. It was announced that the Motorcycle Division's losses amounted to over £8 million. Share value fell to just $7^1/_2$p, from a 1971 figure of 87p. One London newspaper commented that, "BSA had managed to snatch disaster from the jaws of success".

The Research and Development centre at Umberslade Hall was closed down early in 1972, and selected staff were drafted back to Meriden. By this time, Lord Shawcross had become Chairman of the Board and announced that all the group's 500 and 650cc motorcycles would now be built at Meriden, with all other projects being shelved for the time being. Unfortunately, this directive was never implemented, and the two factories struggled on with a redundancy-depleted workforce.

Late in 1972, Mr Dennis Poore, Chairman of Norton Villiers Ltd., started discussions with BSA/Triumph and the government in an attempt to save the motorcycle industry. In march 1973, the Government was informed by the Minister of State that proposals for a new motorcycle company comprised of Norton Villiers and BSA/Triumph had been accepted. By the middle of the year, the new company, Norton Villiers Triumph Ltd., had been formed, with the Department of Trade and Industry (DTI) injecting £4.8 million into the venture. As the Triumph factory closed for the annual two week holiday, everyone looked forward to a secure future.

All was not what it seemed, though. Bert Hopwood, who had been appointed responsible for the final design at Meriden, resigned within one month of his appointment, and Poore announced that the Triumph factory was to close, and that all motorcycle production would be at BSA's Small Heath site. This announcement led to the workers taking over the Meriden factory from the 14th September 1973.

The Triumph factory remained closed for eighteen months until the workers' co-operative was set up, and Triumph motorcycles were produced again at Meriden.

Unfortunately, the Triumph Engineering Co. Ltd. brand name had been sold off separately, so the new title, Meriden Motorcycles, had to be registered by the co-operative.

Meriden Motorcycles operated until 1983 but was never well funded, working very much on a day to day basis with no money for development.

Finally, in 1983, Meriden Motorcycles was wound up by the liquidators, and all remaining stock, machine tools, jigs and fixtures went under the hammer. The site was sold separately and is now a desirable housing estate. The Triumph name lives on, however, as the avenues are called Bonneville Close and Daytona Drive!

Chapter 2
The Triumph Trophy

The origins of the Trophy TR5 go back as far as 1940, when the company produced a lightweight 349cc twin (3TW) for the British Army. This machine was made to a Ministry specification which, among the many stipulations laid down, stated that it must be of light weight, start easily, give 10,000 miles service and be cheap to produce. Triumph met all these conditions bar the last.

The 1940 3TWD 350cc machine incorporated three firsts for Triumph: an AC alternator for lighting, a high-level siamezed exhaust system, and aluminium was used for both the cylinder head and the barrel. Dry weight was a commendable 230lb. Note the stressed fuel tank replacing the top frame tube.

The Triumph Trophy Bible

The 3TWD in its production form featured a modified gearbox and front forks, and the alternator was relocated to the primary chaincase.

To meet the Ministry condition on weight, Triumph used a lot of expensive aluminium - cylinder barrel, cylinder heads, mudguards, and even the rider's footrests were all alloy - and this drove up the cost accordingly.

It's uncertain how many of these 3TW models were produced for the British Army (most sources quote a maximum of 50, though). It's thought that some found their way to France during WWII, but were destroyed or left on the beaches upon the retreat from Dunkirk. What is certain, however, is that those remaining in the Coventry factory were totally destroyed when the city was blitzed on 14th November 1940.

One example still remains, however, though how and why it has survived has never been explained. It was overhauled in the Triumph Service Department and loaned to the National Transport Museum (where it still resides).

In the immediate post-war period, as I have mentioned already, there were many difficulties for the company, and the country, to overcome. As well as the steel and electricity rationing already referred to, there was also a great shortage of fuel. Rationing was in force across the country, but, luckily for Triumph, a small amount of petrol was available for competition use, in the interests of development.

Committed to producing only twin cylinder models for the early post-war period, the company was faced with a problem concerning the choice of machine for competition use. It could hardly use the 250/350cc Tiger single cylinder models that had been so successful in competition before the war. So, to show faith in the new products, it had to be a twin.

A study of the model range showed that the Speed Twin and Tiger 100 would be much too big and heavy for one-day trials use, which only left the 349cc 3T. Fortunately, the 3T converted quite readily to a one-day trials machine, and became quite successful in the capable hands of Messrs. Alves, Jefferies and Gaymer, the works riders of the day.

A glance at the accompanying photos will show that the 3T trials was far from being a super works special. Its only non-standard parts were the 21 inch front wheel, trials tyres, siamezed exhaust system, and handlebars to suit the rider. Wide ratio gears were fitted to the gearbox, and the overall ratios were lowered by the use of a 17 tooth engine sprocket. The engine remained completely standard, and even used the cast iron cylinder barrel and head.

The 3T trials was a winner, though. Ridden by PH (Jim) Alves, it won the 1946 Cotswold Cup national trial on its first outing. Jim confounded the critics by taking two more premier awards in national trials, the Mitchell and the Beggars Roost. He would have made the tally four but for a bit of bad luck. In the Bemrose Trophy trial, a previous rider knocked down a section of a wall, in the period between Jim inspecting the section and riding it. Taking the path he had mentally noted, he was suddenly confronted by a huge pile of rocks through which there was no possible path. The bike stopped dead, stuck on the rocks, and Jim lost five marks and the premier award.

Many thought that the works had concocted something special in the engine, for it stood to reason, the experts argued, that no twin cylinder machine could give the same amount of wheel grip as a single. It was

The Triumph Trophy

thought, therefore, that these wins were probably some kind of fluke. However, Mr Alves went from strength to strength, winning many more national trials against some of the world's best trials riders.

Due to Jim's success, there was soon a full works team participating in all the major trials. PH Alves, as mentioned; Alan Jefferies, an older, pre-war Triumph rider; and AF Gaymer, one of the new boys of the post-war era.

The works 3T trials machine changed little for 1947,

The 1946/47 works 3T Trials. A standard 3T petrol tank has been fitted for the photo session.

The Triumph Trophy Bible

Triumph was so pleased with Percival 'Jim' Alves' win that this advert was placed in 1946.

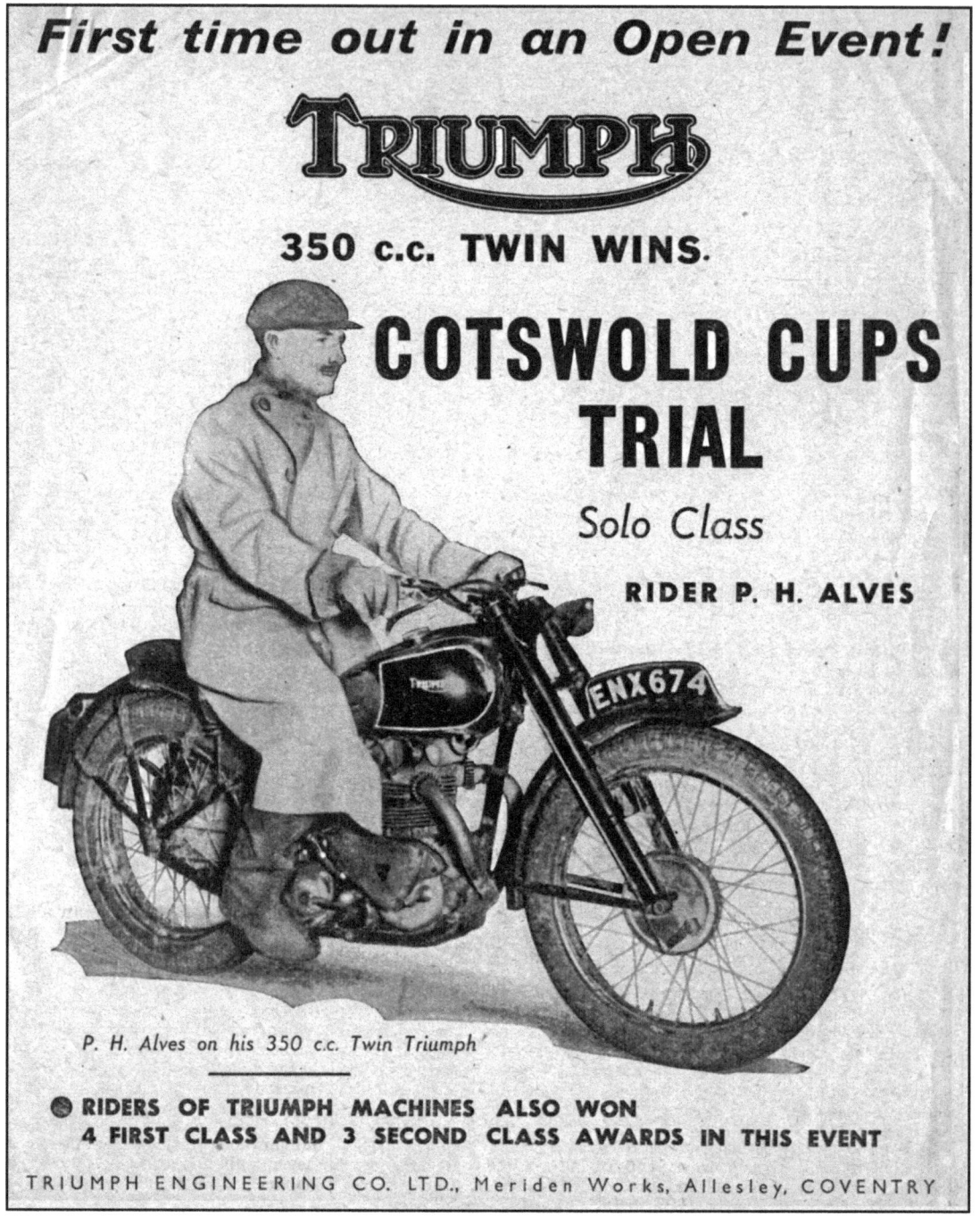

the only changes being lighter, narrower mudguards, siamezed upswept exhaust, and an aluminium cylinder barrel and head borrowed from the four cylinder generator set (two 3T engines coupled together to give 700cc). This barrel and head should not be confused with the later Trophy TR5 units which came from the twin cylinder generator set.

With the works riders doing so well, it wasn't long before the company started getting orders for "a bike like the one ridden by Mr Alves". Under this kind of pressure, instructions were given to the design department to come up with a production version of the 3T trials.

In true Triumph tradition this was soon accomplished using as many standard items as possible, the theory being that newly designed parts cost money for tooling. At least one complete machine was produced to the designed specification, and was titled the 3TR.

There is no doubt that it would have made quite a good competition bike at that time. Having ridden both 3T trials and a TR5 in trials trim I can vouch that

The Triumph Trophy

Following on from the Cotswold win, Triumph advised that it could not yet supply an 'Alves' replica. It never would, of course.

the 3T was much more controllable, due to the softer power delivery.

However, having almost reached the production stage, it was announced that the 1948 International Six Days Trial (ISDT) would be held at San Remo in Italy, and Triumph decided to participate.

The decision to enter the ISDT meant that the company's thinking regarding a competition trials bike had to change. Triumph knew that the 17bhp of the 3T would be found wanting in an International Six Days Trial type event (it had used the T100 in pre-war International Six Days Trials, so knew what was required). Furthermore, whilst domestic success was all very nice, international participation had a greater potential for generating sales. It was soon decided, therefore, that a 500cc machine was required.

The competition department took delivery of three Speed Twins, and fitted them with the aluminium

The Triumph Trophy Bible

A Drawing Office-designed Trials model that nearly went into production. It's fitted with an alloy cylinder head taken from the 700cc four cylinder generator engine. Note the valve lifter cable entering the exhaust tappet block.

The Triumph Trophy

Triumph's first 500cc trials machine. The Speed Twin engine with generator set cylinder head is squeezed into a 3T frame. The fuel tank is a pre-war Tiger 70 unit, and the tin chaincase is taken from an ex-WD 3HW. Jim Alves used this machine during 1947/48.

alloy cylinder barrel and head to give better cooling and lighter weight. Smaller, three gallon, petrol tanks, narrower sports mudguards and trials tyres completed the transformation.

In what was widely acknowledged as the toughest International Six Days Trial to date, with very hot dusty conditions and numerous rocky outcrops, the three modified Speed Twins did exceptionally well. Alves, Jefferies and Gaymer each gained gold medals, and together won a manufacturer's team award for Triumph.

This was one of the two manufacturer's awards presented that year - the other went to the Czechoslovakian team riding Jawa machines.

At an 'inquest' after the event, the riders voiced the opinion that the general handling needed sorting out, and that the bikes were generally too big and cumbersome. It was suggested that something like the 3T trials bike, but with a 500cc engine, would be more suitable. Taking note of these comments, and realising that an International Six Days Trial type machine may be more in keeping with the growing US market requirement, where enduro type events were becoming popular, the firm set to and produced what was glibly termed a replica of the winning 1948 machines. The firm obviously wanted to trade on the success of the win, so it stretched the truth a little. This, in fact, did no harm, since no International Six Days Trial Speed Twin replicas had been offered for sale, and the reworked/redesigned machines were much better than the original San Remo Speed Twins.

Thus the TR5 evolved, and what other name could it carry but 'Trophy', in recognition of the sterling performance of the Speed Twins of 1948. The new TR5

The Triumph Trophy Bible

Trophy sales brochure for 1950.

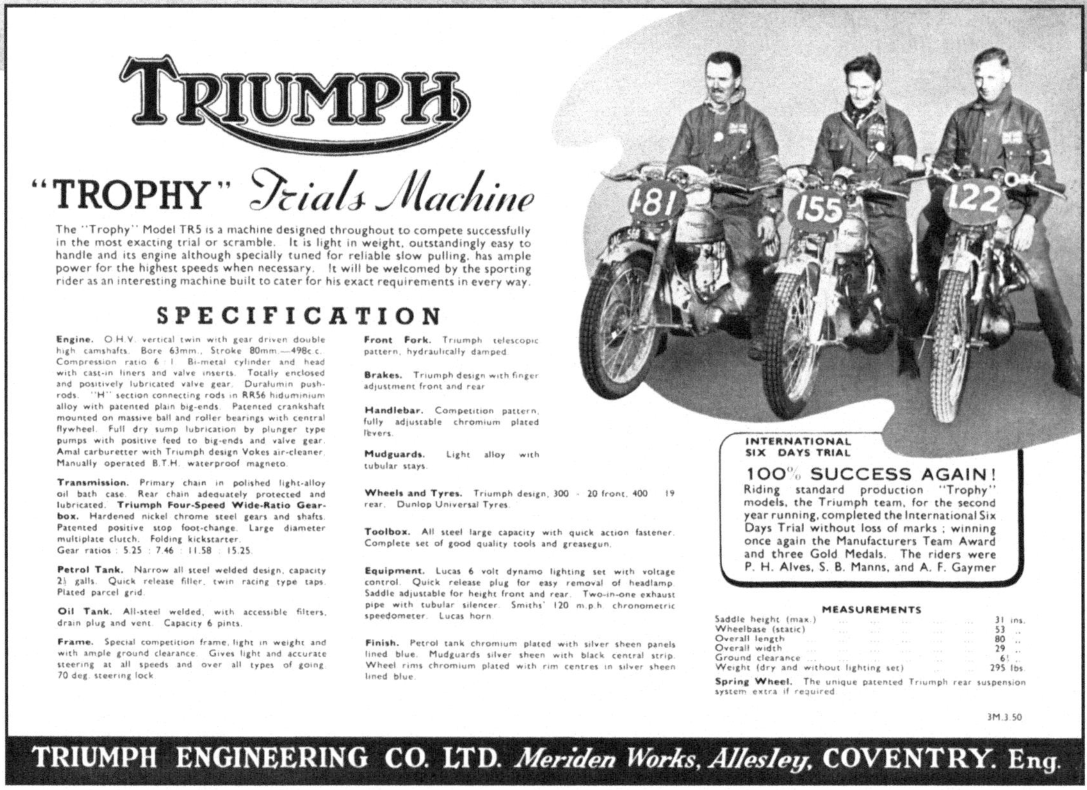

TRIUMPH
"TROPHY" *Trials Machine*

The "Trophy" Model TR5 is a machine designed throughout to compete successfully in the most exacting trial or scramble. It is light in weight, outstandingly easy to handle and its engine although specially tuned for reliable slow pulling, has ample power for the highest speeds when necessary. It will be welcomed by the sporting rider as an interesting machine built to cater for his exact requirements in every way.

SPECIFICATION

Engine. O.H.V. vertical twin with gear driven double high camshafts. Bore 63mm., Stroke 80mm.—498c.c. Compression ratio 6 : 1. Bi-metal cylinder and head with cast-in liners and valve inserts. Totally enclosed and positively lubricated valve gear. Duralumin pushrods. "H" section connecting rods in RR56 hiduminium alloy with patented plain big-ends. Patented crankshaft mounted on massive ball and roller bearings with central flywheel. Full dry sump lubrication by plunger type pumps with positive feed to big-ends and valve gear. Amal carburetter with Triumph design Vokes air-cleaner. Manually operated B.T.H. waterproof magneto.

Transmission. Primary chain in polished light-alloy oil bath case. Rear chain adequately protected and lubricated. **Triumph Four-Speed Wide-Ratio Gearbox.** Hardened nickel chrome steel gears and shafts. Patented positive stop foot-change. Large diameter multiplate clutch. Folding kickstarter.
Gear ratios 5.25 : 7.46 : 11.58 : 15.25.

Petrol Tank. Narrow all steel welded design, capacity 2½ galls. Quick release filler, twin racing type taps. Plated parcel grid.

Oil Tank. All-steel welded; with accessible filters, drain plug and vent. Capacity 6 pints.

Frame. Special competition frame, light in weight and with ample ground clearance. Gives light and accurate steering at all speeds and over all types of going. 70 deg. steering lock.

Front Fork. Triumph telescopic pattern, hydraulically damped.

Brakes. Triumph design with finger adjustment front and rear.

Handlebar. Competition pattern, fully adjustable chromium plated levers.

Mudguards. Light alloy with tubular stays.

Wheels and Tyres. Triumph design, 3.00 - 20 front, 4.00 - 19 rear. Dunlop Universal Tyres.

Toolbox. All steel large capacity with quick action fastener. Complete set of good quality tools and greasegun.

Equipment. Lucas 6 volt dynamo lighting set with voltage control. Quick release plug for easy removal of headlamp. Saddle adjustable for height front and rear. Two-in-one exhaust pipe with tubular silencer. Smiths' 120 m.p.h. chronometric speedometer. Lucas horn.

Finish. Petrol tank chromium plated with silver sheen panels lined blue. Mudguards silver sheen with black central strip. Wheel rims chromium plated with rim centres in silver sheen lined blue.

INTERNATIONAL SIX DAYS TRIAL
100% SUCCESS AGAIN !
Riding standard production "Trophy" models, the Triumph team, for the second year running, completed the International Six Days Trial without loss of marks ; winning once again the Manufacturers Team Award and three Gold Medals. The riders were P. H. Alves, S. B. Manns, and A. F. Gaymer.

MEASUREMENTS
Saddle height (max.)	31 ins.
Wheelbase (static)	53 "
Overall length	80 "
Overall width	29 "
Ground clearance	6½ "
Weight (dry and without lighting set)	295 lbs.

Spring Wheel. The unique patented Triumph rear suspension system extra if required.

3M.3.50

TRIUMPH ENGINEERING CO. LTD. *Meriden Works, Allesley,* **COVENTRY.** Eng.

The Triumph Trophy

Although the advert proclaims a 1951 win on the new model, the picture shows Jim on a much earlier model.

1948, 1950 and now 1951!

AGAIN WINS

COLMORE CUP TRIAL

Rider - - P. H. ALVES

THE FIRST MAJOR EVENT IN WHICH THE 1951 TROPHY MODEL WITH ITS NEW ENGINE HAS APPEARED

A characteristic photograph of the 1951 Colmore winner and his Trophy Triumph, taken in an earlier event.

Won by Triumph for the Third Time in Four Years!

(Subject to official confirmation)

TRIUMPH ENGINEERING CO. LTD., MERIDEN WORKS, ALLESLEY, COVENTRY

The Triumph Trophy Bible

A nice attempt at giving the Trophy swinging arm rear suspension. Built for the Belgian distributor in 1952.

was fitted with the same engine as the 1948 models except that the compression ratio was lowered to 6.0:1. This, of course, could be altered by fitting pistons from the 5T or T100, so ratios of 7.0:1 or 7.7:1 were available. A wide ratio gearbox was normally specified as standard, but again, a standard or even close ratio gearbox could be fitted.

The TR5 was fitted with narrow section aluminium alloy mudguards with tubular stays, and standard Triumph hubs were laced into 20 inch WM1 and 19 inch WM3 rims

The Triumph Trophy

Ever popular, especially with the girls, Steve McQueen poses on his TR6 prior to the 1964 ISDT. This picture was taken on the front lawn at Meriden.

carrying Dunlop 3.100 inch x 20 inch and 4.00 inch x 19 inch Trials Universal tyres. A 2½ gallon petrol tank and a small Lycett spring seat gave the Trophy a real business-like look. So much so, in fact, that some Triumph buffs swear it was the best looking Triumph ever produced.

The first public appearance for the Trophy was at the Earls Court motorcycle show in November 1948. This motorcycle was strictly a pre-production job, for it was not until mid-January the following year that the model started to roll off the assembly line.

That Triumph had a winner was demonstrated by the fact that the 1948 International Six Days Trial success was repeated in each of the next three years. It was very nearly four but, in the 1952 event, John Giles had the misfortune of holing a piston during the speed test on the last day, and he took silver instead of gold. The Trophy's light weight and good spread of power made it a wonderful long distance machine, and in certain American events it had no peer. It certainly started a trend, and it wasn't long before most of the rival factories in Britain followed suit by using a twin cylinder model for International Six Days Trial events. It's fair to say, though, that none seemed to have the charisma of the Trophy, and none were true production models, as the Trophy certainly was.

That the Trophy was also a versatile motorcycle soon became widely recognised. The ordinary clubman could use his machine for his everyday commitments,

Bud Ekins collects his 1962 TR6 from the factory. Bud went on to win a gold medal in the Garmisch Parten-Kirchen ISDT.

19

The Triumph Trophy Bible

Triumph staff discuss the 1957 Trophy TR5. Left to right: Doug Magano, Jack Wicks, John Nelson and Ivor Davies. The picture was taken on the front lawn at Meriden, and the factory can be seen in the background.

and then, come the weekend, could participate in a local trial or scramble. This all-round performance may have concealed the fact that the Trophy was not among the best one day trials machines. It required considerable skill and throttle control to find the ultimate wheel grips, and steep muddy descents could be distinctly hazardous as little engine braking was available.

It's interesting to note that the latter problem must have been discussed when the 3TR was being designed, for the drawings show it would have featured an exhaust valve lifter. This took the form of a wedge fitted into a special exhaust tappet block, and controlled by a Bowden cable and a handlebar-mounted lever. Tension on the cable moved the wedge which, in turn, held up the cam-followers and so kept the exhaust valves open.

From its conception in 1948 to the end of production in 1954, the basic Trophy changed only slightly. One of the most obvious changes was the introduction of the close fin die cast cylinder barrel and cylinder head for the 1951 season. This change harmonised the Trophy and the Tiger 100 engine components. A less obvious change was the introduction of a stronger gearbox in 1950. Originally introduced for the 650cc Thunderbird, it was harmonised throughout the range. Easily recognised by the speedo cable connection in the right side casing, this was a much stronger, and therefore reliable, gearbox.

The spring hub rear suspension had been offered as an optional extra from 1949. In 1950, this was upgraded to the MkII version. However, this unit found little favour with the competition boys due to the fact that it added around 20lb to the weight of the machine, and it couldn't be quickly removed in the event of a puncture, for example.

For the 1955 season, the Trophy joined all the other Triumph twins in using a swinging-arm rear suspension. In some ways this increased the Trophy's versatility, but the light rigid model of earlier years had now gone. The works riders had used the new swing-arm frame in the 1953 International Six Days Trial, so the mechanics were well sorted by the 1955 production date.

It would be fair to say that the new frame gave the Trophy a new lease of life, in so far as it dominated the desert races in the USA. Quite often, the first five or ten finishers in a race would be Trophy-mounted. Riders of the calibre of Bud Ekins, his brother Dave, Steve McQueen, Lee Marvin, and a host of others competed regularly in these desert races - all using the Triumph Trophy, of course.

The factory still catalogued the Trophy in trials trim for 1955, but it was now only available to special order. The new model really didn't suit the British one day trials, though, as it had gained quite a few pounds in weight and a few inches on the wheelbase, both being a severe handicap. One had to admire John Giles, however, who rode his works Trophy right up until 1958. John was a twin man, and was very successful, but during the last few years the company threatened to confiscate his beloved Trophy in favour of a 200cc Tiger Cub. John eventually had to bow to the inevitable, and his Trophy was pensioned off and dismantled when he was issued with the little Cub. I don't believe John enjoyed his trials riding so much after that.

For the 1956 season, the TR5 500cc Trophy was joined by its bigger brother, the TR6 650cc. This TR6 (Trophy-Bird in US parlance), was introduced primarily for the American market, and was aimed mainly at the enduro and cross-country events that were so popular there.

A typical event of this kind was the Big Bear, America's toughest trial. The Big Bear was run over two 75 mile laps of rough tracks in the Mojave desert, where riders had to content with steep hills, gullies, and even snow at times. The course was so punishing for the riders and machines that, in some years, only 70 or 80 riders finished the course. However, the difficulties did not deter people from entering the event. In fact, by the end of the 1950s, it was not uncommon to have over 900 starters!

From this very brief description it will be appreciated that just to finish the race, let alone win, was quite an achievement. That the Trophy was well featured at the end of the race showed how well it performed, and how well suited to this type of event it was. Indeed, so good was the new Trophy-Bird TR6, that the three absolutely stock models which were entered for the 1956 Big Bear Run, finished first, second and third. Leading the entire race, Bill Postel, Bud Ekins and Arvin Cox only had to decide amongst themselves who would win. Looking at the Big Bear results for 1956, 1957 and 1958, it would seem that one had to be Trophy-mounted to stand any chance of success:

1956 - first four places, and six in the first ten finishers.
1957 - first twelve places, and twenty in the first twenty-five finishers.
1958 - first five places, and eight in the first ten finishers.

Cycle-wise, the 649cc Trophy was similar to the TR5, but adopted the engine from the Tiger 110 to get the increased capacity. It featured an aluminium alloy

The Triumph Trophy

Factory adverts proclaiming wins in the USA.

cylinder head and a cast iron cylinder barrel, the latter painted silver for cosmetic symmetry (a black painted barrel looked out of place, and gave the impression of being heavy). It was surprising how many owners assumed that the cylinder barrel was aluminium, but it was not the company's intention to fool them. The overall gearing was raised to make full use of the 40bhp that was available.

It would be no exaggeration to say that the TR6 was one of Triumph's most popular models. It found favour with the desert racers, and, at the other end of the spectrum, the rider who wanted a sports model but didn't want the hassle of the twin carburettor Bonneville.

For the 1958 season, Triumph introduced the auto clutch, otherwise known as the 'Slick Shift'. This device enabled the rider to change gear with the foot change pedal which operated the clutch at the same time. It was one of Triumph's poorer innovations. I never found anyone who had a kind word for it.

The front brake on the TR6 was now of the full width pattern, with the 8 inch diameter being retained. This modification added a few pounds to the unsprung weight with little or no benefit to the braking. It did, however, harmonise the front brake drums across the range.

The next major change to the Trophy TR6 was the introduction of a new frame for the 1960 season (easily recognisable by the twin front downtubes, and known as the duplex frame). Also new for 1960 was the use of a crankshaft-driven alternator housed inside the primary chaincase. Battery charging was through a full wave rectifier.

The new frames started breaking, however, almost as soon as the new Trophy hit the dirt in the USA, with the two front downtubes fracturing just under the steering head lug. Absolutely no indication of this failure had manifested itself during the thousands of miles the prototypes had covered. This embarrassing failure was soon corrected by the addition of a lower tank rail, but not before a costly warranty rework had been undertaken.

It was around this period that the model code gained an extra letter. UK bikes were plain TR6, but the US models, due to the different specifications, were dubbed TR6C, TR6R, TR6SC, and, for 1960 only, TR6A and TR6B. Very generally, a rough breakdown of the models is as follows:

TR6 Standard Dunlop K70 tyres, flat UK handlebars, three gallon petrol tank, standard ratio gearbox and siamezed upswept exhaust system. Later, the TR6 featured a four gallon petrol tank and twin, low level exhaust system.

TR6C Dunlop's Trials Universal or Dunlop Sports tyres, wide semi-upswept handlebars, three gallon petrol tank, wide ratio gearbox and siamezed upswept exhaust system. Later, the model featured two upswept pipes on the left side.

TR6SC Basically a stripped TR6C. Dunlop Sports tyres, semi upswept handlebars, three gallon petrol tank, standard ratio gearbox (optional wide ratio), long, straight-through upswept exhaust pipes, one each side, energy transfer direct ignition systems. TR6SC production was limited, and all went to Jomo (Johnson Motors) on the West Coast of the US.

TR6SR This model was the US equivalent to the UK TR6.

The Triumph Trophy Bible

A Triumph advert for Christmas 1948. The bikes are Speed Twins modified for the 1948 ISDT.

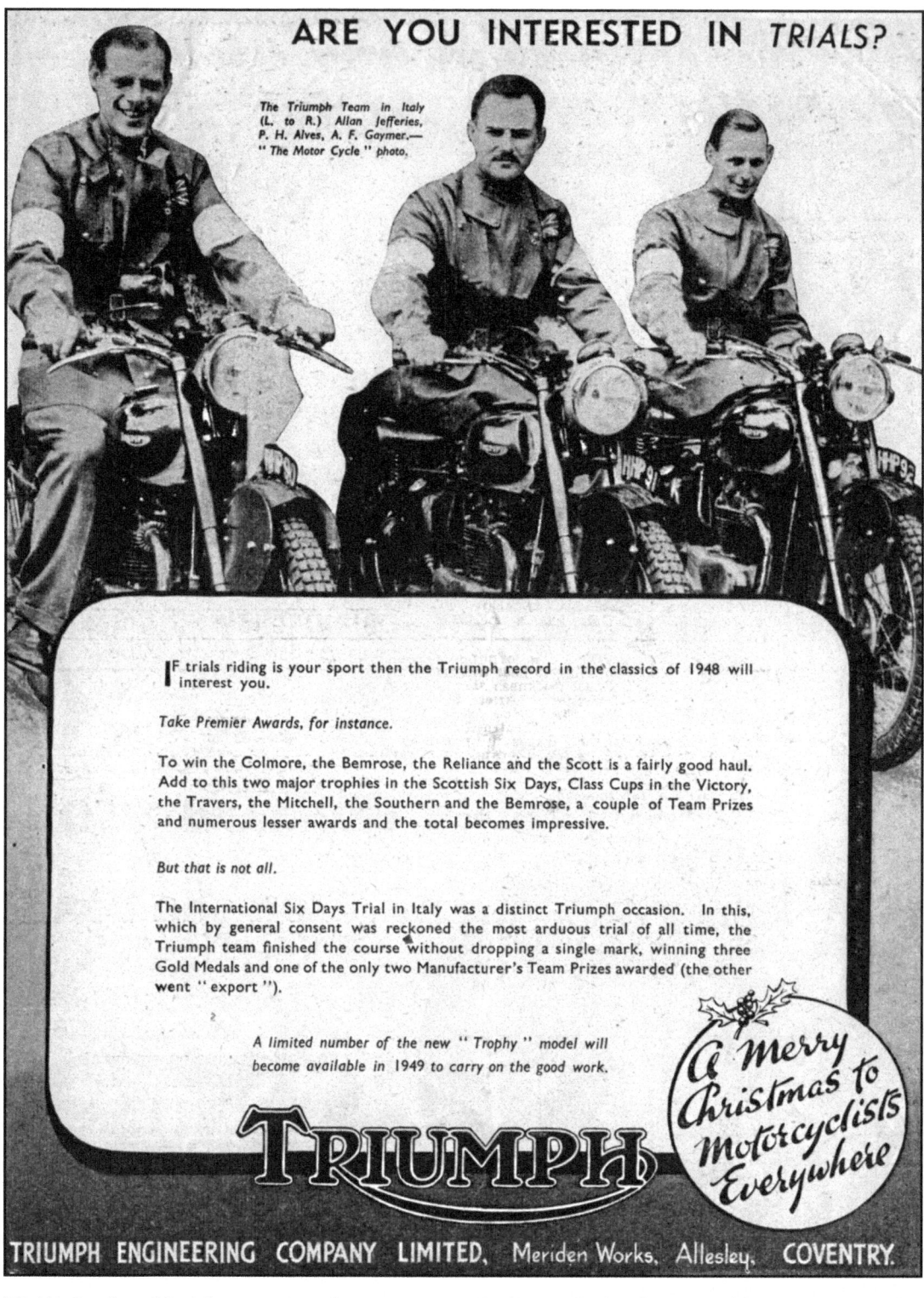

TR6/A Dunlop ribbed front tyre, Dunlop K70 rear, upswept US handlebars, three gallon petrol tank, standard ratio gearbox, twin low level exhaust pipes and barrel type silencers. Usually fitted with a tachometer driven from the timing cover.

TR6/B Dunlop Trials Universal front tyre and Dunlop Sports rear tyre, upswept handlebars, standard ratio gearbox, three gallon petrol tank, twin high level exhaust pipes and small barrel-type silencers. Mainly exported to Tri-Cor (Triumph Corporation) on the US East Coast.

The Triumph Trophy

Triumph sets a record which, most likely, still stands amongst British manufacturers.

TR5A/C Dunlop Trials Universal tyres, upswept handlebars, wide ratio gearbox, 2½ gallon petrol tank, siamezed low level exhaust system on the right hand side, energy transfer direct ignition and lighting.

TR5A/R Dunlop 19 inch ribbed front tyre, Dunlop 18 inch K70 rear tyre, upswept handlebars, three gallon petrol tank, standard ratio gearbox, twin low level exhaust pipes and barrel silencers, standard coil ignition electrical system.

Both the TR5A/R and A/C used the 490cc unit construction engine from the T100A, and were produced exclusively for Tri-Cor and Jomo. Although only in the

'Bert' Gaymer, with his hat on back to front, on his way to a gold medal in the 1951 event.

The Triumph Trophy

sales line-up for one year, the TR5A/R and A/C paved the way for the T100C models which would continue into the next decade.

In the late 1960s, the TR6 Trophy had lost its competition influence, and became merely a single carburettor Bonneville. This was emphasised by the fact that both bikes had identical camshafts and pistons.

Bob Manns gained a gold medal in the 1949 ISDT riding this bike.

The Triumph Trophy Bible

1950 Trophy ridden by Jim Alves in the 1950 ISDT. A map case on the petrol tank, compressed air bottle fixed to the rear frame, reversed centre stay on the front mudguard, tommy bars on the wheel spindles, spare throttle slide in a container under the manifold, and spare wheel spokes taped to the mudguard stay, are all the bits that make an ISDT bike special.

International Six Days Trials

One of the major annual events that the Triumph company took seriously was the International Six Day Trial (ISDT). This event, as the name implies, consisted of six separate days' trials, over a different course each day. Riders rode against the clock, checking in at numerous points along the route. If a rider checked in outside his time allowance, time marks would be deducted. For a gold medal to be gained, a clean sheet at the end of the six days was required. It was usual for the trial to be run over rough mountain tracks and linking tarmacadam roads, so, as fairly high average speeds were needed to keep on schedule, a rider with stamina and a reliable machine was required. ISDT riders needed a good degree of mechanical expertise, too, as outside assistance was barred and exclusion could be the penalty if any was detected.

The first ISDT was held in Cumbria in 1913, but Triumph did not feature largely until the mid-1930s. The introduction of the Tiger models saw Triumph taking the event seriously, with the Tiger 100 being used just prior to WWII.

Post-war, the ISDT resumed with the 1947 event held in Czechoslovakia. However, as the regulations had arrived late and seemed to favour the small capacity machines (of which most of the continental teams consisted), the British manufacturers declined to take part. Of the three private entries from Great Britain two were Triumph twins, ridden by JA Hitchcock and AA Sanders. The latter retired on the first day due to numerous punctures and running out of time. Hitchcock managed to get to the last day before the bearings in the spring hub failed.

The 1948 event was held at San Remo in Italy and resulted in a brilliant win for Triumph. Riding modified Speed Twins, the team of Alan Jefferies, 'Jim' Alves and Bert Gaymer won gold medals and took the manufacturer's team prize. For the 1949 event, 'proper' TR5 Trophy models were used, with the same riders as the previous year. Again, gold medals and manufacturer's awards resulted, and this was the case for the next two years.

For the 1953 event, Triumph fielded fully sprung Trophy models, featuring the newly-introduced swinging arm frame specified for the 1954 T100 and T110 only. This shows up two main points. Firstly, the competition department must have had great faith in the design and development of the new frame, and secondly, the team was desperate for a machine with rear suspension as all the rival factories had it by now. It's pleasing to report that 'comp shop' faith was fully justified, and no frame breakages were experienced.

As the ISDT progressed in the post-war period, various rule changes took place. To take advantage of these changes, Triumph fitted 650cc Thunderbird engines to some Trophy TR5 models from 1951.

Factory machines, via the 'comp shop', continued to be available to the works riders, and, therefore, for selection to represent Great Britain and the manufacturer's team. Generally, machines were used for about two ISDTs, the exception being where the production model changed visually so the competition department had to be seen to be using current production models.

This situation continued until 1965 when the parent company, BSA, decided that the 'comp shop' at Meriden would be closed down. The long standing rivalry between the two factories had really come to a

The Triumph Trophy

To take advantage of the ISDT regulations, Triumph fitted a 650cc Thunderbird engine to a basic TR5. This one was ridden by Jim Alves in the 1952 event.

The Triumph Trophy Bible

A TR5 built for the 1953 ISDT tests in Wales. In the actual ISDT, swinging arm rear suspension machines were used.

head in the 1965 ISDT, when all the BSA works entries had retired, whilst Triumph won gold medals and a manufacturer's team prize.

For the 1966 ISDT, the ACU ruling body declared that, due to the poor showing of BSA in 1965, it was going to choose an all Triumph team for the event. This rankled with BSA, and the reply to the ACU was that if BSA was not considered, no Triumphs would be available!

A compromise was eventually worked out, though, whereby the machines would be BSA, but powered by Triumph engines. The bad news for Meriden, though, was that all the machines would be built at BSA Small Heath!

Aware of the ill feeling between the two companies, and with the 'crystal ball' in overdrive, Triumph reopened the 'comp shop' and, very secretly, refurbished the 1965 ISDT bikes, and added four new ones to the stable, not trusting the agreed compromise. On the eve of the 1966

The Triumph Trophy

For the 1953 ISDT, Triumph used the swinging arm frame. This prototype shows a non-standard seat, front mudguard and silver finish.

The Triumph Trophy Bible

Jim Alves' 1953 ISDT 650cc TR5. Note the alternator-type primary chaincase and parallel tube silencer.

The Triumph Trophy

For the 1954 ISDT, the factory mounts were fitted with eight inch front brakes.

The Triumph Trophy Bible

Jim Alves' 1954 ISDT machine. The Tiger 110 650cc engine predates the Trophy TR6 by a couple of years. Note the eight inch front brake, reinforced footrests and repositioned centre stand pivots.

ISDT selection tests, BSA reported to the ACU that, due to other pressing commitments, it had only completed one of the six machines promised. Whether BSA ever intended to comply with the ACU request is open to discussion, but, on the face of it it's unlikely, since BSA then suggested using the failed B40 and Victors of the previous year, albeit reworked.

One suspects that this blatant ploy upset the ACU folk, so much so, in fact, that they contacted Triumph to enquire if the previous year's bikes could be made available. Triumph's gleeful answer was to say that, not only were last year's bikes refitted and ready to go, but it had, just by chance, of course, four new ones that could be offered.

During the selection tests, the BSA-Triumph hybrid was assessed by the riders, and all except one BSA works rider declared it to be seriously lacking in development

The Triumph Trophy

A factory advert showing the swinging arm frame for all 1955 models. The inset shot shows a youthful Ken Heanes on his Trophy TR5.

for the job in hand. So, for the actual 1966 ISDT event, Triumph fielded six bikes, while there were only two of the BSA/Triumph hybrids. It's nice to report that all won gold medals with the Triumph, two squads each gaining manufacturer's team awards. However, this reliability went against Triumph, as BSA lost a manufacturer's team award when the BSA Victor, which made up the team with the BSA hybrids, expired.

This debacle sealed the fate of further works participation in ISDT events for both factories. When it was announced that the 1967 trial would be held in Poland, BSA refused to take part, nor was it prepared to loan or sell any of the previous year's bikes. For Triumph, this saw the end of a golden age of successful participation

The Triumph Trophy Bible

John Giles shows off his new 1956 TR6 ISDT mount. The photograph was taken on the rear lawn at Meriden.

The Triumph Trophy

The 1958 ISDT machines featured full width front brakes, direct lighting, TR6-type cylinder heads, and single seats.

The Triumph Trophy Bible

Although a member of the BSA group, Triumph still put out its own adverts.

in long distance events which would be hard to equal. Triumph now relied on dealer sponsored or private entries for the ISDT events, but this met with limited success, not so much due to the quality of the bikes, however, but rather to the event regulations favouring the smaller capacity continental two-stokes.

The next works entries from the Triumph factory was in 1973, when the machines were TR5T Adventurers. The 1973 event was held in the Berkshire Mountains of Massachusetts, USA. The bikes used were taken from

The Triumph Trophy

The 1966 BSA/Triumph hybrid. Prepared by the BSA Competition Department, this was basically a Victor with a Triumph engine.

stock in the US warehouse of Duarte. Modifications included Betor front forks with QD front wheel, BSA B40 type QD rear wheel, plastic mudguards, and smaller head and tail lights. The ignition system was simplified by the use of a Lucas Capacitor System with dual back-up.

Eight of the TR5Ts were modified for American

The Triumph Trophy Bible

A 1973 TR5T as ridden by the British team in the 1973 ISDT in America.

and British team riders, and proved quite reliable (the only mechanical failure was a broken fork stem). The British team won a silver medal, coming second to the Czech CZ factory team.

Chapter 3

Technical development

1949 TR5 Trophy

Engine prefix: TR5
Frame numbers: TC 11001T to TC 13107T
Engine numbers: 9106001 to 9112671
Build dates: 18-10-1948 to 27-09-1949
Engine number prefixed by figure 9 to identify 1949 season build

Engine The TR5 engine specification closely followed the well established T100 of 1946. In the interest of better cooling and reduced weight, though, the cylinder barrel and cylinder head were of aluminium rather than the cast iron of the T100.

Squarish in shape, the alloy barrel and head were exactly as those used on Triumph's wartime generator set, except that the cowling fixing bosses were not drilled and threaded. Incidentally, the generator set was originally supplied to the Royal Air Force. Mounted on a two wheel trolley, it could be run out to the aircraft to charge the batteries *in situ*.

The vertical twin overhead valve gear was operated by high camshafts working in phosphor bronze bushes inside an aluminium alloy crankcase.

The crankshaft consisted of a right and left crankweb bolted to a central flywheel by six high tensile bolts. The crankshaft assembly was supported inside the crankcase by a twin-lipped roller bearing on the timing side, and a ball journal bearing on the drive side.

Plain bearings were used for the big ends, with white metal fused to the lower steel end caps. The upper half of the bearing was machined directly from the forged hiduminium alloy of the con rod. The small end of the connecting rod was fitted with a bronze bush to act as a bearing for the steel gudgeon pin.

The aluminium alloy cylinder barrel incorporated cast-in iron liners and threaded bosses for the cylinder head retaining bolts.

The cylinder head was also of aluminium alloy, with a cast-in spectacle-shaped insert for the valve seats and the spark plug boss. Exhaust ports were internally threaded to take castellated exhaust pipe retainers.

Dry sump lubrication was maintained by a plunger pump driven by the inlet camshaft. Pressure was controlled by a release valve screwed into the timing cover, with an oil pressure indicator button incorporated. Oil feed to the rockers and overhead valve gear was by a take-off on the return side of the oil tank, via a small metal pipe.

Aluminium alloy pistons, with a compression ratio of 6.0:1, featured two plain compression rings and one oil control ring. The gudgeon pin had a parallel bore and was retained in the piston by round wire circlips.

Valves had $^5/_{16}$ inch diameter stems, and the head diameters were identical at $1^5/_{16}$ inch, though only the heads of the inlet valves were tulip-shaped. Both inlet and exhaust valve guides were of chilled cast iron, with the exhaust being the longer of the two.

Ignition was provided by a flange-mounted BTH magneto situated at the rear of the cylinders, and gear-driven from the inlet camshaft. Advance and retard of the ignition was via a cable to a control lever on the left-hand side of the handlebars.

The direct current 45 watt dynamo was a separate unit, mounted in front of the cylinders, and gear-driven from the exhaust camshaft pinion.

An Amal 276-type carburettor supplied the fuel mixture, with the float chamber mounted on the left-hand side. The choke was operated from the right-hand handlebar-mounted control lever via a Bowden cable. The twistgrip was of Triumph's own design, being progressively geared to give a variable throttle opening from tickover position. Friction control was via a spring loaded knurled knob on the twistgrip body.

Gearbox The gearbox was Triumph's own design and manufacture, and, unless specially requested, was fitted

The Triumph Trophy Bible

1949 Trophy TR5. For 1949 and 1950, the Trophy featured the square barrel and head from the wartime generator set.

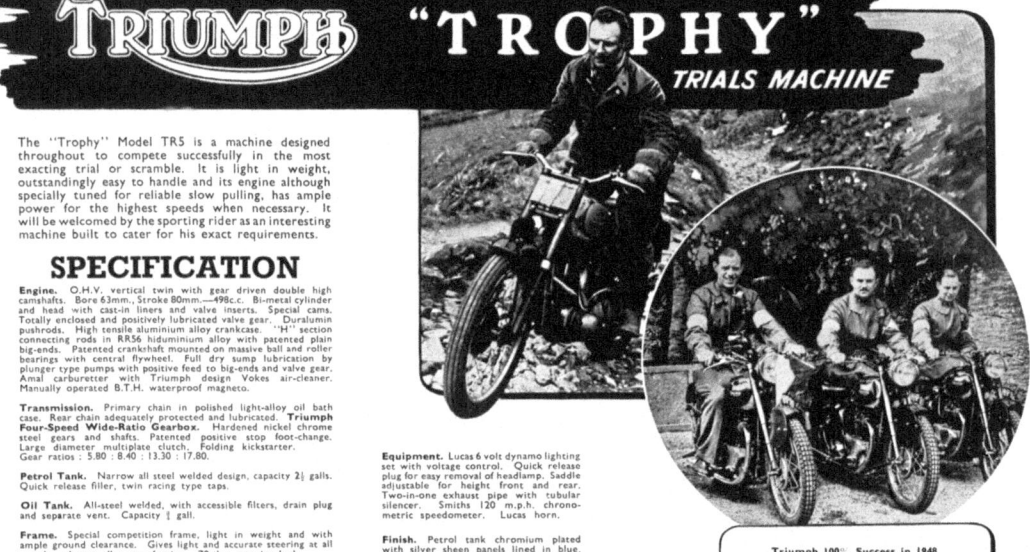

TRIUMPH "TROPHY" TRIALS MACHINE

The "Trophy" Model TR5 is a machine designed throughout to compete successfully in the most exacting trial or scramble. It is light in weight, outstandingly easy to handle and its engine although specially tuned for reliable slow pulling, has ample power for the highest speeds when necessary. It will be welcomed by the sporting rider as an interesting machine built to cater for his exact requirements.

SPECIFICATION

Engine. O.H.V. vertical twin with gear driven double high camshafts. Bore 63mm, Stroke 80mm.—498c.c. Bi-metal cylinder and head with cast-in liners and valve inserts. Special cams. Totally enclosed and positively lubricated valve gear. Duralumin pushrods. High tensile aluminium alloy crankcase. "H" section connecting rods in RR56 hiduminium alloy with patented plain big-ends. Patented crankshaft mounted on massive ball and roller bearings with central flywheel. Full dry sump lubrication by plunger type pumps with positive feed to big-ends and valve gear. Amal carburetter with Triumph design Vokes air-cleaner. Manually operated B.T.H. waterproof magneto.

Transmission. Primary chain in polished light-alloy oil bath case. Rear chain adequately protected and lubricated. **Triumph Four-Speed Wide-Ratio Gearbox.** Hardened nickel chrome steel gears and shafts. Patented positive stop foot-change. Large diameter multiplate clutch. Folding kickstarter. Gear ratios : 5.80 : 8.40 : 13.30 : 17.80.

Petrol Tank. Narrow all steel welded design, capacity 2½ galls. Quick release filler, twin racing type taps.

Oil Tank. All-steel welded, with accessible filters, drain plug and separate vent. Capacity ⅝ gall.

Frame. Special competition frame, light in weight and with ample ground clearance. Gives light and accurate steering at all speeds and over all types of going. 70 deg. steering lock.

Front Fork. Triumph telescopic pattern, hydraulically damped.

Brakes. Triumph design with finger adjustment front and rear.

Handlebar. Competition pattern, fully adjustable chromium plated levers.

Mudguards. Light alloy with tubular stays.

Wheels and Tyres. Triumph design wheels, 300 × 20 front, 400 × 19 rear. Dunlop Universal Tyres.

Toolbox. All steel large capacity with quick action fastener. Complete set of good quality tools and greasegun.

Equipment. Lucas 6 volt dynamo lighting set with voltage control. Quick release plug for easy removal of headlamp. Saddle adjustable for height front and rear. Two-in-one exhaust pipe with tubular silencer. Smiths 120 m.p.h. chronometric speedometer. Lucas horn.

Finish. Petrol tank chromium plated with silver sheen panels lined in blue. Mudguards in silver sheen with black central strip. Wheel rims chromium plated with rim centres in silver sheen lined blue.

Measurements.
Saddle height (max.) ... 31 ins.
Wheelbase (static) ... 53 ,,
Overall length ... 80 ,,
Overall width ... 29 ,,
Ground clearance ... 6½ ,,
Weight (dry and without lighting set) ... 295 lbs.

Spring Wheel. The unique patented Triumph rear suspension system available as an extra if required.

Triumph 100% Success in 1948 INTERNATIONAL SIX DAYS TRIAL Riding 500 c.c. Triumph Twins, Allan Jefferies, P. H. Alves and A. F. Gaymer completed the course without loss of marks, winning three Gold Medals and the only Team Prize awarded to a British manufacturer. Allan Jefferies also captained the victorious British Trophy Team and P. H. Alves was a member of the winning British Silver Vase Team (Top photo) **P. H. Alves on his Triumph Twin.** Winners of the following classic "Open" Trials since the war :—The Colmore Cup, West of England, Cotswold Cups, Bemrose, Reliance, Mitchell, Traders Cup, Scott Trial and many others.

TRIUMPH ENGINEERING COMPANY LIMITED, Meriden Works, Allesley, COVENTRY, ENGLAND.

EM549

Technical development

with a set of wide ratio gears. Selection of the gears was through a positive stop right side foot control. Shafts and gears were nickel chrome steel housed in a separate alloy casing from the engine, and pivoted on the bottom fixing bolt to allow primary chain adjustment. The mainshaft and high gear ran on ball journal races, whilst the layshaft had a mixture of cast iron and phosphor bronze bushes.

Primary transmission This was by .305 inch x $\frac{1}{2}$ inch chain from the engine sprocket to the clutch sprocket, and was housed in a cast alloy oil bath. The shock absorber was incorporated in the engine sprocket/mainshaft assembly, and consisted of a spring-loaded face cam.

The clutch was a multi-plate affair, with alternate steel and corked plates, with four pressure springs controlling the drive. Clutch operation was via a rod through the mainshaft to a lever on the right side of the gearbox, and then via a cable to the left-hand-mounted handlebar lever. A small rubber cover covered the cable nipple at the gearbox lever.

Frame The frame was special to the TR5, and was unlike any other in the Triumph range. To get a short wheelbase, the front down-tube stopped off just above the dynamo, and a fabricated box-section engine plate assembly then connected this to the lower engine tubes. Forged lugs were used on the frame assembly, into which tubes were pinned and brazed.

The main frame consisted of tank and seat tubes, with a tapering front down-tube. Twin tubes running under the engine and gearbox were joined by a pair from the saddle nose at the rear wheel spindle.

A rear stand was fitted, pivoting just below the wheel spindle. It was retained in the up position by a large spring anchored to the pillion footrest.

Suspension Front suspension was by Triumph-designed hydraulically-damped telescopic forks. The forks had six inches of movement and featured internal springs.

Rear suspension was optional, but when specified was by a spring wheel.

Petrol tank An all welded steel construction with a capacity of $2\frac{1}{2}$ imperial gallons. It featured a distinctive front mounting, in the form of two 'ears' jutting forward to take a single fixing bolt. A quick release hinged filler cap was fitted, and two bosses were provided to accept the petrol taps.

Exhaust system This was unique to the Trophy. The pipes were made in one piece, with the threaded fixing nuts fitted during the assembly. The right-hand pipe was siamezed into the left, which was then routed along the top of the chaincase. The pipe then terminated into a parallel tubular silencer.

Oil tank All welded steel construction with a capacity of 6 imperial pints. It was fitted with an aluminium screwed filler cap.

Wheels Triumph-designed fabricated steel hubs. Front - pressed drum with brazed on spoke flange. Rear - cast iron drum with bolted on steel sprocket. Seven inch diameter brakes front and rear, of single leading shoe design, with cast alloy front anchor plate and a steel pressing for the rear.

Tyres Dunlop Trials Universal were the specified tyres, 3.00 x 20 inch front and 4.00 x 19 inch rear.

Mudguards Painted alloy mudguards with tubular stays attached to the mudguard by small individual clips, nuts and bolts.

Air filter A Vokes rectangular filter, with an angled rubber connection to the carburettor intake, fitted between the oil tank and the battery carrier.

Handlebars $\frac{7}{8}$ inch diameter, semi-raised to give good control in cross-country conditions. The left side was fitted with the clutch and ignition control levers, dipper switch and ignition cut out button, while the right side had the twistgrip, brake lever, horn button and air control lever.

Toolbox A triangular pressed steel toolbox with hinged lid was attached to the rear frame tubes. A dzus fastener in the lid gave access to the tool kit.

Saddle A Lycett Aero Elastic or Terry spring saddle with chrome plated parallel seat springs. Special long spring fixing studs were fitted, giving a range of seat heights.

Speedometer A Smiths chronometric speedometer with a plain black and white dial. Smiths' code was S491/3 for the 120mph unit, and S491/7 for the 180kph one.

The speedo drive was from the rear wheel as standard, but, when fitted with the optional spring wheel, the drive was taken from the gearbox sprocket.

Electrical A BTH D152/AC9 magneto with manual spark control supplied the ignition. A Lucas 40 watt dynamo, type E3HRD, was originally fitted, but, from TC 13001 (22/6/1949), this was replaced by a Lucas 60 watt unit (E3L-LI-O). Battery charge was regulated by a Lucas MCR-2-L voltage control unit.

The headlamp was fitted with a multi-pin plug making the wiring harness quickly detachable.

Transfers

Minimum oil level	Gilt
Drain/refill, *etc.*	Gilt
Recommended lubricants	Gilt
Rear number plate	Gilt/white

Positions: Drain and refill - on front face of oil tank followed by recommended lubricants reading across the tank. Minimum oil level - approximately halfway up the tank. The rear number plate transfer was 'Triumph', with the registered design number placed between the lower fixing bolt holes.

Price £195.11.8.

The Triumph Trophy Bible

Extras
Pillion footrests	£1.0-4
Pillion seat	£1.11-9
Speedometer	£5.1-8
Spring wheel	£20.6-5
Luggage grid	£1.11-9
Prop stand	£1.11-9

1949 TR5 Trophy

Engine
Bore	63mm/2.480in
Stroke	80mm/3.15in
Capacity	498cc/30.4 cu in
bhp (max)	24 @ 6000rpm
Compression ratio	6.0:1

Cylinder head
Material	aluminium alloy
Valve seat angle	45 degrees
Valve seat width	
Inlet	0.050/0.060in
Exhaust	0.060/0.080in
Valve guide bore	0.498/0.4985in

Valves
Stem diameter	
Inlet	0.3095/0.3100in
Exhaust	0.3090/0.3095in
Head diameter	$1^{5}/_{16}$in
Valve O/A length	$3^{55}/_{64}$in

Valve guides
Material	Chilled cast iron
Bore diameter	0.3120/0.3130in
Outside diameter	0.5005/0.5010in
Length	
Inlet	$1^{31}/_{32}$in
Exhaust	$2^{11}/_{64}$in

Valve springs
Free length - nominal	
Inner	$1^{5}/_{8} \pm {}^{1}/_{16}$in
Outer	$2^{1}/_{32} \pm {}^{1}/_{16}$in
Fitted length	
Inner	1.187in
Outer	1.281in

Cam follower
Foot radius	0.750in
Stem diameter	0.3110/0.3115in

Valve clearance - cold
Inlet	0.002in
Exhaust	0.004in

Valve timing (checked with zero tappet clearance)
IVO	BTDC $26^{1}/_{2}$ degrees
IVC	ABDC $69^{1}/_{2}$ degrees
EVO	BBDC $61^{1}/_{2}$ degrees
EVC	ATDC $35^{1}/_{2}$ degrees
Valve lift	0.294in

Push rods
Material	tubular steel
Overall length	6.300/6.325in

Rockers
Bore diameter	0.5002/0.5012in
Spindle diameter	0.4990/0.4995in

Camshafts and bearings
Journal diameter	
Left-hand	0.8100/0.8105in
Right-hand	0.8730/0.8735in
End float	0.013/0.020in
Lobe height	1.047/1.055in

Bush diameter
Left-hand bore	0.8125/0.8135in
Right-hand bore	0.874/0.875in
O/A length	
Left-hand inlet	1.000/1.010in
Left-hand exhaust	0.932/0.942in
Right-hand	1.010/1.020in

Cylinder barrel
Material	aluminium alloy
Liner	cast iron
Cylinder bore	2.4800/2.4805in
Tappet block bore	0.9985/0.9990in

Tappet block
Material	aluminium alloy
Outer diameter	0.9995/1.000in
Tappet stem bore	0.3120/0.3125in

Piston rings
Ring gap fitted	
Compression ring	0.010/0.014in
Scraper ring	0.010/0.012in
Ring thickness	
Compression ring	0.062/0.0625in
Scraper ring	0.124/0.125in
Clearance in piston groove	
Compression ring	0.001/0.003in
Scraper ring	0.001/0.0025in

Pistons
Diameter at skirt	2.4760/2.4765in
Gudgeon pin bore	0.6882/0.6885in

Connecting rod
Big end diameter	1.4375/1.4385in
Small end diameter	0.6890/0.6894in
Length between centres	6.499/6.501in
Side clearance fitted	0.012/0.016in

Small end bush
Material	phosphor bronze
Outer diameter	0.8140/0.8145in
Length	1.030/1.031in

Crankshaft
Crankpin diameter	1.4360/1.4365in

Technical development

Main bearing journal diameter
    Drive side (LH)   1.1247/1.1250in
    Timing side (RH)   0.9997/1.000in
    Crankshaft end float   0.003/0.017in
    Oil feed journal diameter   0.622/0.623in
    Balance factor   52%

Crankshaft bearing
    Drive side
        Ball journal RMS9   1.125 x 2.812 x 0.812in
    Timing side
        Roller RM10 LL   1.00 x 2.50 x 0.750in

Crankshaft oil feed bush
    Internal diameter   0.6245/0.6255in

Oil pump
    Feed plunger diameter   0.3122/0.3125in
    Scavenge plunger diameter   0.4371/0.4374in
    Feed bore   0.3125/0.3127in
    Scavenge bore   0.4371/0.4374in
    Spring length   1/2in
    Ball valve diameter   7/32in

Oil pressure release valve
    Pressure release   65lb
    Spring length   1 1/8in

Carburettor
    Type   Amal 276 DK/1A
    Main jet   150
    Needle jet   0.107in
    Needle   Type 6
    Needle position   3
    Throttle valve   6/3 1/2
    Bore   15/16in

Ignition
    BTH magneto
        Timing   3/8in fully advanced
        Points gap   0.012in
        Spark plug   L105 Champion
        Plug gap   0.018in
        Thread size   14mm
        Reach   1/2in

Transmission
    Clutch
        Corked plates   4
        Plain plates   5
        Pressure springs   4
        Spring free length   1 1/2in
        Bearing rollers   20
        Bearing diameter   0.2495/0.2500in
        Bearing length   0.231/0.236in
        Clutch sprocket bore   1.8745/1.8755in
        Clutch hub bearing dice   1.3733/1.3743in
        Clutch rod diameter   7/32in
        Clutch rod length O/A   11 3/4in

Kick-start mechanism
    Inner case bore diameter LH   0.6245/0.6255in
    Bush bore diameter RH   0.751/0.752in
    Spindle diameter RH   0.748/0.749in
    Spindle diameter LH   0.6215/0.6225in
    Ratchet sleeve O/D diameter   0.8747/0.8752in
    Ratchet spring free length   1/2in

Gearchange mechanism
    Quadrant plunger
        Outer diameter   0.4315/0.4320in
        Plunger bore   0.4325/0.4330in
    Plunger spring
        Number of coils   12
        Free length   1 1/4in

Footchange spindle
    Diameter LH   0.6238/0.6241in
    Diameter RH   0.7488/0.7491in
    Bush bore LH   0.6245/0.6255in
    Bush bore RH   0.7495/0.7505in

Quadrant springs
    Number of coils   12
    Free length   1 3/4in

Camplate plunger
    Plunger diameter   0.4360/0.4365in
    Housing bore   0.4375/0.4380in
    Spring length   2 1/2in
    Number of coils   19

Mainshaft
    Main bearing LH   1 1/4 x 2 1/2 x 5/8in ball journal, RL59Z with chip shield
    Bearing RH   3/4 x 1 7/8 x 9/16in ball journal, RLS6
    Mainshaft diameter LH   0.8098/0.8103in

Layshaft
    Bearing diameter LH/RH   0.560/0.5605in
    Bush bore diameter LH/RH   0.562/0.563in
    Bush outer diameter LH/RH   0.688/0.689in
    Layshaft sleeve bush   1 3/8in x 0.7493/0.7500in

Number of teeth on pinions

Layshaft		Mainshaft
17	4th	27
21	3rd	23
26	2nd	18
29	1st	15

Sprockets
    Engine   21
    Clutch   43
    Gearbox   18
    Rear wheel   46

Gear ratios internal
    4th   1.00
    3rd   1.45
    2nd   2.30

	1st	3.07

Overall ratios
	4th	5.24
	3rd	7.60
	2nd	12.02
	1st	16.08

Chains
	Primary	$5/16$in x $1/2$ x 76 link
	Secondary	$3/8$in x $5/8$in x 90 link

Wheels
	Rims	
	Front	WM1 x 20in
	Rear	WM3 x 19in
	Tyres	Dunlop
	Front	3.00 x 20in Universal Trials
	Rear	4.00 x 19in Universal Trials
	Security bolts	
	Front	1 WM1
	Rear	1 WM3

Brakes
	Diameter	7in
	Width - lining	$1 1/8$in

Bearings
	Front hub - ball journal	20 x 47 x 14mm (6204)
	Rear hub - taper roller	$9/16$ x $1 3/4$ x $3/16$in 3K1163 / 3K1120N1
	Rear spring hub MkII	$3 1/2$ x 5 x $3/4$in Ball journal

Spokes
Front	Front	Rear
N/S L/H	10 x $9 3/8$ x 10G	20 x $8 3/4$ x 9G
N/S L/H	10 x $9 3/8$ x 10G	
O/S R/H	10 x $7 15/16$ x 10G	20 x $8 3/4$ x 9G
O/S R/H	10 x $7 15/16$ x 10G	
Spring hub 19in 40 x $5 5/16$ x 8/10G		

Wheel offset
	Front	Drum edge to centre of rim: $2 3/16$in
	Rear	Outer edge of sprocket to centre of rim: $3 5/32$in
	Spring hub	Central to spoke flanges

Steering head bearings
	Top	22 x $3/16$in ball
	Bottom	20 x $1/4$in ball

Front forks
	Stanchion diameter	1.3025/1.303in
	Top bush internal diameter	1.3065/1.3075in
	Bottom bush outer diameter	1.4935/1.4945in
	Top bush O/A length	0.995/1.005in
	Bottom bush O/A length	0.870/0.875in
	Fork leg bore	1.498/1.500in
	Spring free length	$19 1/4 \pm 3/16$in
	Spring wire diameter	0.160in (8swg)

Electrical
	Dynamo	Lucas E3H RD 40 watt
	Voltage regulator	Lucas MCR-I-L
	Earth	negative
	Battery	Lucas 6v 12amp PUL7E/4
	Horn	Lucas HF 14/41 ALTETTE
	Head lamp	Lucas DU 42
	Tail lamp	Lucas MT10
	Bulb main	6v 24/30 or 24/24
	Bulb pilot	6v 3w
	Bulb speedo	6v 3w
	Bulb tail	6v 3w

Speedometer
	Type	Smiths S491/3/L 120mph, 1500 plain dial

Dimensions
	Wheelbase	53in
	Overall length	80in
	Overall width	29in
	Seat height	31in
	Weight dry	295lb
	Ground clearance	$6 1/2$in

Capacities
	Petrol tank	$2 1/2$ gallon (11.4 litres)
	Oil tank	6 pint (3.4 litres)
	Gearbox	$3/4$ pint (450cc)
	Primary case	$1/4$ pint (150cc)
	Front forks	$1/6$ pint (100cc)

Lubrication
	Engine	SAE 20-50
	Gearbox	EP 90
	Primary case	SAE 20
	Grease	Castrol LM
	Forks	SAE 20

Torque settings
	Con-rod nuts	28lbft
	Fly wheel nuts	12lbft
	Cylinder head bolts	18lbft
	Camshaft pinion nuts	50lbft
	Crankshaft pinion nut	50lbft
	Engine sprocket nut	80lbft
	Clutch shaft nut	50lbft
	Kick-start ratchet nut	30lbft
	Gearbox sprocket nut	80lbft

Left-hand threads
Camshaft pinion nuts.

1950 TR5 Trophy

Engine prefix: TR5

Technical development

Engine and frame numbers: 1118N to 16101N
Build dates: 18.10.1949 to 03.11.1950

Reference to the year of manufacture within the engine number was deleted. It had been causing embarrassment to overseas dealers who, on occasions, were still selling the previous season's models, due to the interval between manufacture and delivery to dealer's showrooms.
The engine and frame numbers now matched each other, and ran concurrently with the rest of the models in the Triumph range.

Engine The oil pump feed plunger diameter was increased, giving 20% greater flow. Redesigned connecting rods with through bolts and self lock nuts replaced fixed studs and top-mounted castellated nuts secured by split pins.

Gearbox A completely redesigned gearbox was introduced and harmonised throughout the range. It was considered that the original gearbox would not be adequate for the newly introduced 650 Thunderbird.

The new gearbox had a much stronger, live one-piece layshaft. Provision for the speedo drive was incorporated in the gearbox inner cover, via a 90 degree angle from the layshaft. Layshaft bearing diameters increased, and the bushings changed from cast iron to sintered bronze. The redesign also provided for a garter type oil seal on the final drive sprocket.

The new gearbox had different internal ratios due to the gear teeth alterations:

4th	1.00
3rd	1.425
2nd	2.21
1st	2.915

Gearbox gears - number of teeth

Layshaft		Mainshaft
18	4th	28
22	3rd	24
27	2nd	19
30	1st	16

Overall ratios

4th	5.24
3rd	7.46
2nd	11.58
1st	15.25

with the continued use of a wide ratio gear cluster.
Layshaft bush bore diameter: 0.6865/0.6880in.
Layshaft journal diameter: 0.6845/0.6850in.
Note that none of the gears or shafts are interchangeable between the old and new type gearboxes.

Transmission No change.

Frame No change, but a crankcase undershield was specified from 3027N (7.12.1949).

Petrol tank The tank luggage rack was now fitted as standard.

Oil tank No change.

Brakes No change.

Wheels
Front: No change.
Rear: The MkII springwheel with a WM3 x 19in rim was fitted from 9345N (25.5.1950) as an optional extra.

Mudguards No change.

Exhaust system No change.

Air filter No change.

Electrical No change.

Speedo
Smiths 491/3. 120mph 1500 plain dial, drive cable 44in o/a length.

Handlebars No change.

Saddle No change.

Toolbox No change.

Price £200.13.3.

Extras
Pillion footrests	£1.0.4.
Pillion seat	£1.11.9.
Speedometer	£5.1.8.
Springwheel	£20.6.5.
Propstand	£1.11.9.

1951 TR5 Trophy

Engine prefix: TR5
Engine and frame numbers: 101NA to 14934NA
Build dates: 3.11.1950 to 5.11.1951

New NA suffix to engine and frame number.

Engine A new die-cast aluminium alloy close pitch finned cylinder barrel and cylinder head was specified to harmonise with the Tiger 100 model. The cylinder barrel now featured pressed in cast iron liners and bosses for the cylinder head fixing bolts. The new cylinder head carried larger inlet valves, at $1^7/_{16}$in from $1^5/_{16}$in, with the exhaust remaining at $1^5/_{16}$in.

Duralumin push rods were specified to match the barrel and head expansion rate. Stellite tipped cam followers were introduced at 13224NA (6.9.1951) to combat premature wear of follower and camshaft lobes.

The stronger connecting rods introduced for the 650cc 6T were now specified for all models. The only change to the pistons was to fit taper-faced piston rings. Camwheels now incorporated three keyways to harmonise with the T100 model. A new fully machined crankshaft with heavier lobweights was used, and the balance factor

The Triumph Trophy Bible

The 1951 Trophy lost the glamorous chrome panelled petrol tank, but gained a new engine.

changed to 64%.

A boxed race kit was offered for the TR5 and T100 for the 1951 engines. Comprising race camshafts, high CR pistons, twin carburettors, remote float chamber, tacho kit and megaphone exhaust, which, when fitted, raised the power to 42bhp (putting it on a par with the old Grand Prix, a 'ready to race' 498cc twin produced between 1947 and 1948). All this for just £35.00.

Gearbox The knurled edge filler cap in the outer cover was replaced by a rocker box inspection cap. This had a hexagon head to aid removal and refitting.

Transmission No change.

Frame The prop stand lug was incorporated into the rear frame assembly, replacing the previous clamp-on type. Also, threaded bosses were added to the chainstay lugs.

Forks The crown and stem was modified to give increased trail.

Petrol tank A Ceandes filler cap of the push and twist cam action replaced the hinged lever type. Lever type taps were now specified.

Technical development

Built to incorporate every refinement required by the competition rider the Triumph "Trophy" model has a long string of successes to its credit from every corner of the world. Easy and accurate to handle, thanks to its light weight (295 lb.) and a steering geometry evolved as a result of experience gained in fiercely contested competitive events. The engine, using the same unique die cast alloy head and barrel as the "Tiger 100," is designed to provide a high power output at low revolutions, yet give adequate top end performance when required. Riding standard "Trophy" models the Triumph team completed the 1950 International Six Days Trial without loss of marks, winning a Manufacturers Team Award—the third to be won in succession (1948-49-50).

SPECIFICATION

O.H.V. vertical twin. Bore 63 mm., stroke 80 mm., 498 c.c. Dry sump lubrication. Air cleaner. Manual control magneto. Two-in-one exhaust. 6" ground clearance. 70° lock. Telescopic forks. Wide ratio four-speed gearbox. 2½ gall. petrol tank. Folding kickstarter. Quick release headlamp. Dunlop tyres 400—19 rear 300—20 front. Finished silver sheen and black. (For complete technical data see back pages.)

PAGE 7

1951 Trophy.

Oil tank A Ceandes filler cap replaced the threaded alloy one and the tank filler neck was modified to suit.

Brakes The front brake drum was of one piece construction, made from Mechenite cast iron. This replaced the pressed drum and welded-on spoke flange, and improved the brake effectiveness.

Wheels No change.

Mudguards No change.

Exhaust system The exhaust pipes were reshaped to accommodate the splayed port cylinder head. This modification necessitated that the pipes now had to be a two part affair to enable assembly.

Air filter No change.

Handlebars No change.

Toolbox No change.

Saddle No change.

Speedometer No change.

Electrical The Lucas 53009A tail lamp was replaced by the 53216A type. The new unit gave provision for the fitting of a stop lamp. Also, the cone-shaped body gave a larger lens.

Price £200.13.13d.

Extras As 1950.

1952 TR5 Trophy

Engine prefix: TR5
Engine and frame numbers: 16000NA to 22000NA then 26046 to 31625.
Build dates: 7.11.1951 to 15.8.1952

After engine and frame number 22000NA, the suffix NA was omitted on all Triumph models except the TRW.

Engine The only change was to the oil pump check valve plugs. These were now castellated to allow a better oil flow.

Gearbox No change.

Transmission No change.

Frame The steering head was changed to give increased trail. The rear brake pedal pad was reduced in size and given a pinnacled finish. The distance between the pivot point and the rear cross bar on the rear stand was increased, since it was found that in certain instances tyre fling could cause fouling.

Forks Fork springs were shortened by .750in in common with other models in the range.

Petrol tank The petrol tank lost its attractive chrome plated finish for this season. The finish was now totally painted in silver sheen, with dark blue lining outlining the shape of the previous panels.

Petrol feed pipes changed to clear PVC, replacing the braided steel ones.

Oil tank The oil tank vent pipe was re-routed to vent into the primary chaincase through a metal pipe with flexible connectors at each end.

Brakes The rear brake drum and sprocket was now integral, replacing the previously separate bolt-on sprocket.

Wheels Wheel rims lost the chrome plated finish due to the severe nickel shortage. Rims were painted silver and retained the dark blue lining.

Mudguards No change.

Exhaust system No change.

Air filter No change.

Electrical A positive earth system replaced the previously used negative earth system.

Speedo No change.

Handlebars No change.

Saddle Only the Lycett saddle was now specified. A redesigned front fixing bracket gave more range of adjustment.

Toolbox No change.

Price £227.8.11.

Extras
Pillion footrest	£1.0.6.
Pillion seat	£1.12.0.
Spring hub	£20.08.11.
Propstand	£1.12.0.

1953 TR5 Trophy

Engine prefix: TR5
Engine and frame numbers: 32854 to 44121
Build dates: 15.9.1951 to 14.9.1953

Engine New camshafts were introduced which incorporated ramps for quieter operation. These camshafts required 0.010in tappet clearance for normal running. Identification was by a spoked wheel stamping mark alongside the engine number. Fitted from engine number 38384 (16.3.1953).

A redesigned crankshaft, with an internal thread to accept a threaded stud to retain the engine sprocket, replaced the previous crankshaft with the external thread on the drive side shaft.

Gearbox The gear change camplate material changed from zinc-based alloy to steel, promoting better wearing properties.

Transmission The engine shaft shock absorber was abandoned, and replaced by a four paddle vane working in eight rubber blocks situated inside the clutch. This modification meant the use of a plain splined engine sprocket with no shock absorber ramps.

Frame The rear number plate was redesigned to take a rectangular tail lamp.

Forks No change.

Petrol tank No change.

Oil tank No change.

Brakes No change.

Wheels Both wheel rims reverted back to pre-1952 condition, *i.e.* chrome with painted centres.

Mudguards No change.

Exhaust system No change.

Air filter No change.

Electrical Suppressers fitted to plug caps. Lucas Diacon 525 rectangular tail lamp fitted. Stop switch now an optional extra.

Speedo No change.

Handlebars No change.

Saddle No change.

Toolbox No change.

Price £227.8.11.

Extras As 1952.

Technical development

1954 TR5 Trophy

Engine prefix: TR5
Engine and frame numbers: 45595 to 52869
Build dates: 7.10.1953 to 6.5.1954

Engine The timing side main bearing was increased to 1.125in x 2.812in x 0.812in, and changed from a twin lipped roller to a Hoffman MSII ball journal. This change required a revised crankshaft with a larger, 1.1247/1.250in right journal. At the same time, the big end journal diameter was increased to 1.6235/1.6240in, with a maximum advised regrind of -0.030in. Balance factor was 52%.

To match the larger crank journals the connecting rod big end diameter was increased to 1.6250/1.6255in.

Gearbox The clutch cable adjuster lug on the gearbox inner cover angle changed to harmonise with the T100/T110 swinging arm suspension models.

Frame No change.

Forks The fork crown and stem stanchion pinch bolts, previously $5/16$in diameter, were increased to $3/8$in diameter to increase rigidity.

Petrol tank No change - see appendix.

Oil tank No change.

Brakes No change.

Wheels No change.

Mudguards No change - see appendix.

Exhaust system The silencer was altered to the teardrop shape.

Air filter No change.

Electrical system A new oblong tail lamp was fitted, giving a larger reflective area. The latest Lucas voltage control box, RB107, was now specified.

Speedo No change.

Handlebars No change.

Saddle No change.

Toolbox No change.

Price £210.0.0.

Extras
Prop stand	£0.18.8
Pillion footrest	£0.19.3
Spring hub	£19.4.0

1954 was the last season of the rigid Trophy, as 1955 models would feature the swinging arm rear suspension. The last TR5 Trophy in rigid form, numbered 52869, was built on 6.5.1954.

The use of the Trophy was changing, especially in the US where enduro riding was the main off-road sport. As some 70% of the total production was being exported to that country, it was only natural that Triumph would pander to the US market.

For the 1955 season, therefore, the Trophy was completely redesigned, and now featured the swinging arm frame which had first been introduced on the Tigers 100 and 110 in 1954.

In keeping with the new enduro image, the engine was uprated with higher compression ratio pistons, sports camshafts and standard ratio gears in the gearbox.

Triumph still listed the TR5 in trials trim, but only to special order. Not many were produced in this condition, though, since, by this time, rival companies were producing stripped and ready to ride one day trials models - something Triumph was unwilling to do.

It would be no exaggeration to say that the Trophy got a new lease of life. With the swinging arm suspension controlled by Girling rear suspension units, it made an ideal cross-country machine. This was ably demonstrated by Messrs. Alves, Hammond and Giles, of course, who each won a gold medal, and gained a manufacturer's team award for Triumph, in the 1954 International Six Days Trial.

In the US, the TR5 and the later TR6 became firm favourites in events such as the Big Bear Enduro, which took place in the Mojave desert and covered over 150 miles of rough hilly terrain. Incidentally, it wasn't unusual to see up to 900 starters in this arduous event! Triumphs usually swept the board, in fact, and, by 1966, Triumphs had won more cross-country championships than all the other makes combined! In 1956, for example, the first twelve riders were Trophy-mounted.

The 1957 Big Bear was won by Bud Ekins on a Trophy TR6, and twenty of the first twenty-five placed finishers were Triumph-mounted. Bud actually went on to become Steve McQueen's stunt man in the film *The Great Escape*, jumping over the barbed wire fences, *etc.*, on a Triumph disguised as a German motorcycle.

1955 TR5 Trophy

Engine prefix: TR5
Engine and frame numbers: 56153 to 69171
Build dates: 23.7.1954 to 27.6.1955

Engine Sports camshafts (E3325) as specified for the Tiger 110 were fitted, along with pistons giving a compression ratio of 8.0:1. The second compression ring was chrome faced, and stronger taper-bore gudgeon pins were specified. A quoted output of 33bhp @ 6500rpm seemed a good increase over the 24bhp produced by the rigid model.

The Amal 276 mixing chamber was as before, but the float chamber was changed to the large TT-type (Amal 302/13), with a top feed.

Tappet blocks and push rod cover tubes were harmonised with the Tiger 100 model, and running tappet clearances were .002in inlet and .004in exhaust.

Timing cover fixing screws were changed to the cross-head posi-drive type.

Gearbox A new main casing was called for, with cast fixing lugs top and bottom, so that the gearbox could be accommodated within the new swing-arm frame. Standard or wide ratio gear clusters could be specified at no extra cost. The inner and outer cover fixing screws were changed to the cross-head posi-drive type.

Primary transmission To accommodate the swing-arm frame, new shorter inner and outer primary chain cases were specified, along with a shorter 70 link chain. A five plate clutch, harmonised with the Tiger 100 and 110, was fitted to transmit the power of the revamped engine. Cross-head screws retained the outer cover.

Frame Although new to the Trophy for the 1955 season, the pivoted fork rear suspension frame had been fitted to the Tiger 100 and 110 for a year, so was reasonably well proven. Girling rear suspension units, with 12.9in between centres, gave 4in of movement at the rear wheel spindle. The 110lb rate springs could be adjusted by a three position cam ring at the lower end of the unit.

Forks Stronger fork springs of 20in length and .168in wire diameter were now specified.

Petrol tank Capacity was increased to three imperial gallons, and the tank was now fixed to the frame by four bolts. Construction was by two half pressings welded together down the centre. The filler cap remained as before, but was now retained to the neck of the tank by a short chain to prevent accidental loss.

Horizontal styling bands were fitted, and retained by the Triumph badge screws. These styling bands were unique to the three gallon tank, being slightly shorter than those on the other models.

Knee grips were retained by shaped plates bolted to the tank via two threaded pommels. The three bar luggage grid was retained.

Oil tank A new oil tank formed a one piece unit with the battery and tool box on the left side. The oil tank was fitted with a large filler cap identical to the petrol filler cap except for the breather hole being deleted. Between the oil tank and battery box was housed the D shaped Vokes air filter.

Brakes No change.

Wheels Front - no change. Rear - the rear wheel was completely new having a much larger wheel spindle and 20 x 47 x 14mm ball journal bearings. A 46 tooth sprocket integral with the brake drum was still used. Brake diameter stayed at 7in, but a new brake anchor plate was fitted with a threaded stud to take the tubular brake torque stay.

An optional extra was the quickly detachable wheel, whereby removal of a through spindle enabled the wheel to be removed from the driving splines leaving the sprocket and brake assembly attached to the frame. On the QD wheel, the bearings were $^3/_4$ x $1^{27}/_{32}$ x $^9/_{16}$in thin taper rollers in the actual hub, and $^7/_8$ x 2 x $^9/_{16}$in (RLS7) ball journal on the sprocket.

On both wheel conditions a WM3 x 18in rim was fitted.

Tyres Dunlop Trials Universal, 3.00 x 20in front and 4.00 x 18in rear, were fitted as standard unless otherwise specified at the time of ordering.

Mudguards Front - as the 1954 model. Rear - a new steel mudguard, of plain D section, was fitted.

Exhaust system The exhaust pipe was reshaped to accept the swing-arm frame, and cupped at the exhaust port end to slide over stubs in the cylinder head. Finned clips were used to retain the pipes. The silencer was as 1954, being teardrop-shaped, but with an altered fixing bracket.

Air filter Common to the other models but new to the Trophy, the air filter was a Vokes D-shaped component, fitted between the oil tank and battery box. The filter had a detachable side cover giving access to the muslin/wire mesh element.

Electrical The quickly detachable headlamp, via plug and socket, was retained, as was the Lucas HF 1441 horn, though it was relocated to the side of the seat nose.

A new Lucas stop/tail lamp (564), incorporating twin integral reflectors and a rubber mounted bulb holder was fitted. A Lucas stop switch (22B 31383) operated directly on the brake pedal lever.

Both Lucas and BTH magnetos were fitted, usually with manual ignition control via a Bowden cable from a handlebar-mounted lever, but, for some markets, mainly the US, automatic spark control was specified.

The last BTH magneto fitted was on 24th March 1955 at 65344.

For the US market, Lucas K2 FR magnetos were specified.

Speedo
S433/3/L 120mph   1630rpm
S433/7/L 180kph   1020rpm

Handlebars A new 1in diameter handlebar replaced the previous $^7/_8$in diameter type. The twistgrip was harmonised with the other models, replacing the previous alloy-bodied unique-to-Trophy type. The handlebar was drilled and threaded on the left side to take the screwed in horn push button.

Clutch and brake levers of 1in diameter were fitted, as were choke and ignition control levers. A chrome magneto cut-out (kill button), and a strap-fitted dip switch completed the handlebar layout.

Saddle A twin seat replaced the single saddle and pillion seat. The twin seat was unique to the Trophy, being slimmer than that fitted to the rest of the range. Seat cover was all black with white piping.

Toolbox Shaped to match the oil tank, the toolbox was

Technical development

combined with the battery box, and the whole unit was covered by a styled lid retained by a recessed screw.

Summary of 1955 TR5 changes

Engine
bhp/rpm	33@6500
Compression ratio	8.0:1
Camshafts	E3325 inlet and exhaust
Timing	IVO BTDC 27 degrees
	IVC ABDC 48 degrees
	EVO BBDC 48 degrees
	EVC ATDC 27 degrees
	(checked with .020in tappet clearance)
Tappet clearance (cold)	0.002in inlet
	0.004in exhaust

Ignition
Timing fully advanced	41 degrees BTC ($^{15}/_{32}$in)
Spark plug	Champion NA10.

Gearbox
Ratios - standard.
Internal		Overall
1.0	4th	5.24
1.19	3rd	6.24
1.69	2nd	8.85
2.44	1st	12.8

Gearbox gears - number of teeth
Layshaft		Mainshaft
20	4th	26
22	3rd	24
26	2nd	20
30	1st	16

Transmission
Clutch
Friction plates	5
Steel plates	6
Pressure springs	4
Spring length	1.969in/1.869in
Primary chain	70 link
Rear chain	100 link

Dimensions
Seat height	305in
Wheelbase	55.7in
Overall length	85.5in
Overall width	28.5in
Ground clearance	5.5in
Weight	365lb dry

Capacities
Petrol tank	3 imperial gallon (13.68 litres)
Oil tank	6 imperial pint (3.6 litres)
Gearbox	1 imperial pint (.6 litres)
Primary case	$^1/_3$ imperial pint (.2 litres)

All nuts and bolts were cadmium plated with the exception of the following, which were chrome plated:

- front fork pinch bolts
- front fork top stanchion nuts
- headlamp retaining bolts
- tank parcel grid fixing screws
- rocker feed dome nuts

Transfers Same as the 1954 model, with the exception of the front engine plate cover. This carried a tappet settings transfer indicating 0.002inlet, 0.004 exhaust.

Price £234.0.0.

Extras
Quickly detachable rear wheel	£3.12.0
Prop stand	£0.18.8
Pillion footrests	£0.19.3

1956 TR5 and TR6 Trophy - Variation TR5/R

Engine prefix: TR5 and TR6
Engine and frame numbers: 70199 to 82797, then 0598 to 0909
Build dates: 8.8.1955 to 27.7.1955

A new engine/frame number series was used towards the end of the season but, more notable for this year was the introduction of the 650cc Trophy TR6 (Trophy Bird), at 70785 on 28.8.1956. The engine was basically the well proven Tiger 110 fitted with an aluminium alloy cylinder head, but retaining the cast iron cylinder barrel, albeit painted in silver.

With a compression ratio of 8.5:1, the 71mm x 82mm engine fitted with the sports camshaft gave 42bhp @ 6500rpm. A fairly flat torque curve made it an ideal cross-country mount, dealing with any conditions and terrain encountered. In the US, Triumph launched the new TR6 by taking three bikes straight from the crates and entering them in the Big Bear enduro (they finished first, second and third). Riders Bud Ekins, Arvin Cox and Bill Postel led the entire race and finished in that order.

From there on, the Trophy held a virtual monopoly on desert racing which would last for the next decade.

Engine Vandervell VP3 shell bearings were fitted to the connecting rod big ends. To maintain the balance factor at 50%, 595 gram balance weights were required as the new con-rods were heavier than before. The TR5 cylinder barrel spigot was reduced in height from $^3/_{16}$in to $^1/_8$in to combat liner cracking. Correspondingly, the cylinder head spigot bore was reduced in depth.

To reduce oil splutter from the engine breather outlet, the inlet camshaft only had one breather hole, fitted from 72123 (22.9.1955).

The TR5 now featured an Amal Monobloc 376/35 carburettor replacing the type 6 Amal.

Monobloc settings.

The Triumph Trophy Bible

IN rugged sporting events in every part of the world, the 500 c.c. Trophy Model (TR5) has earned a wonderful reputation. Designed to be easily adaptable to most forms of motorcycle competition, this year the model is also available with a 650 c.c. engine (TR6), which provides that additional power and speed demanded in the toughest going.

Patent Nos. 475860, 474963, 482024

Bohus Castle, grim sentinel of a past age, near Gothenburg, Sweden.

TR5 and TR6 GENERAL SPECIFICATION

ENGINE. TR5 500 c.c.: TR6 650 c.c. O.H.V. high compression vertical twin with two gear-driven camshafts, "H" section RR56 alloy connecting rods, plain big ends, and central flywheel. Dry sump lubrication, pressure-fed big ends and valve gear. TR5 die-cast alloy head and barrel. TR6 entirely new alloy cylinder head, cast-iron barrel. Air cleaner. Upswept two-in-one exhaust pipe with silencer.

FOUR-SPEED GEARBOX. Positive foot-change, large diameter multi-plate clutch with Neolangite linings and rubber pad type shock absorber.

FRAME. Brazed cradle type frame with swinging arm rear suspension with hydraulic damping adjustable for varying loads.

FORKS. The famous Triumph telescopic pattern with long supple springs and hydraulic damping.

FUEL TANKS. New design petrol tank of reduced width. Ample capacity oil tank. Quick-release caps and accessible filters.

BRAKES. Large diameter cast iron drums, polished front anchor plate, finger adjustment.

WHEELS. Plated spokes and rims; Dunlop Sports tyres optional extra.

ELECTRICAL EQUIPMENT. Powerful chromium-plated headlamp with quickly detachable harness. Lucas 6 volt 60 watt dynamo, automatic voltage control. Lucas "Wader" type magneto.

OTHER DETAILS. 120 m.p.h. (or 180 km.p.h.) Smiths Speedometer; competition type Twinseat; twist grip with adjustable tension; shell-blue sheen and black finish. Safe type ball-ended clutch and brake levers. TR5 available to "TRIALS" specification.

1956 Trophy.

Carburettor	Amal 376/35.
Main jet	220
Pilot jet	25
Throttle valve	$3\frac{1}{2}$
Needle type	C
Needle position	3
Needle jet	.1065
Bore	$\frac{15}{16}$in

To ensure better sealing, from 75058 (12.12.1955), a groove was machined into the carburettor flange and fitted with an 'O' ring.

Gearbox Sintered bronze layshaft bushes replaced phosphor bronze ones as a cost saver.

Transmission The cork inserts on the clutch drive plates were replaced by 'Neo-Langite' pads, bonded directly onto plain steel plates.

Frame The steering head frame lug was fitted with threaded bosses so that the steering stop could be adjusted. The top steering bearing was increased in size, making it the same as the lower one, and using the same quantity of $\frac{1}{4}$in bearings, i.e. 20 top and 20 bottom.

A sidecar fixing lug was added to the bottom of the main seat tube, harmonising the TR5/TR6 with the rest of the range.

Forks The upper fork covers were shortened to finish just under the bottom yoke, and rubber gaiters, retained by steel straps, were fitted.

The end plug of the hydraulic damper tube was redesigned to give more taper, preventing fork bottoming during extreme cross-country use.

Petrol tank The welded ridge down the centre of the tank was fitted with a chrome-plated styling band, and, to give clearance for this, a two bar parcel grid replaced

Technical development

The full width, seven inch front hub was fitted to the 1957 Trophy TR5.

the three bar unit.

A modification to the rear tank mounting bracket, making it fully rubber insulated, was specified in order to reduce tank fractures in that area.

Oil tank No change.

Brakes No change.

Wheels Plain chrome wheel rims were fitted to all models.

Mudguards No change.

Exhaust system No change.

Air filter No change.

Electrics For the TR5, the headlamp was increased in size to 7in, and the chrome plated headlamp shell carried a sealed beam light unit. The wiring harness was still quickly detachable at the lamp by a multi-pin and socket. This modification harmonised the TR5 with the TR6.

A new combined dipper and horn switch with chrome plated cover replaced the separate items. Lucas 'Wader' magnetos were fitted as standard. A competition magneto was an optional extra.

Speedo No change.

Handlebars A new handlebar was specified, deleting the threaded hole that housed the horn button. A new clutch lever bracket was used to mount the combined horn and dipper switch.

Seat No change.

Toolbox No change.

Price £240.0.0.

Extras
  QD wheel   £3.12.0
  Prop stand   £0.18.8
  Pillion footrest   £0.19.3

1956 TR6

Engine
  Bore   71mm (2.79in)
  Stroke   82mm (3.23in)
  Capacity   649cc (40cu.in)
  Compression ratio   8.5:1
  Valve head diameter - in. $1^{19}/_{32}$in
  Valve head diameter - ex. $1^{7}/_{16}$in
  Ignition timing   38 degrees btc
  bhp   42 @ 6500rpm

Carburettor
Amal 289
  Bore $1^{1}/_{16}$in
  Main jet   200
  Needle jet   .107
  Throttle valve   4
  Needle position   3
  Needle type   29
Carburettor after 71634 (13.9.1955)
  Monobloc   Amal 376/40
  Main jet   250
  Pilot jet   25
  Needle jet   .1065
  Throttle valve $3^{1}/_{2}$
  Needle position   3
  Needle type   C

Transmission
  Engine sprocket   24 teeth.
  Primary chain   70 link $^{1}/_{2}$in x $^{5}/_{16}$in
  Rear chain   101 link $^{5}/_{8}$in x $^{3}/_{8}$in
  Gear ratio   4.6, 5.5, 7.8, 11.2
  Weight   380lb

1956 TR5R

Engine and frame numbers: TR5 76113 to TR5 76224

Build dates: 7.1.1956 to 24.4.1956

The Trophy TR5R came into being at the request of the US distributors. Prior to its introduction, entries for the Daytona races had been modified Tiger 100 models. This modification meant quite a lot of work before the bike was suitable. What was required was a ready made racer that could be sold and used straight from the packing crate - a tuned Trophy was the obvious answer.

The US market-only TR5R was based on a normal swing-arm Trophy. However, it sported a 'Red Seal' engine, which meant that it was fitted with twin carburettors, race type camshafts, high compression pistons, *etc*. Each engine was bench tested before installation certifying a minimum bhp. To make the best use of the tuned engine, downswept exhaust pipes terminating in a pair of open megaphones were fitted.

Engine
Compression ratio	9.0:1
Cam followers	$1\frac{1}{8}$in radius
Valve guides	bronze
Camshafts	E3134
Valve springs-white spot	Interference
Magneto	Lucas race type
Magneto pinion	steel
Twin carbs	Amal 276, remote float
Approximate bhp	40 @ 7000rpm

Gearbox
Standard ratio
Heavy duty clutch springs
Steel clutch spring adjuster nuts

Price $947 in US.

1957 TR5 and TR6 Trophy

Engine prefix TR5 and TR6
Engine and frame numbers: 0944 to 011471
Build dates: 23.8.1956 to 26.9.1957

Engine Single keyway camshaft pinions were fitted, reverting back to the 1950 pattern. A timing cover with built-in tacho drive taken from the exhaust camshaft pinion nut was offered as an optional extra. The compression ratio on the TR6 was lowered from 8.5 to 8.0:1.

Gearbox To counter oil leaks between the mainshaft and high gear, the high gear bush was lengthened to protrude into the primary chaincase through the sliding plate, so that any seepage was directed into the chaincase.

Frame From 09382 (9.7.1957), the patented Triumph easy lift centre stand was fitted. The Girling suspension units were fitted with metalastic bushes at the upper and lower ends for reliability.

The swinging arm had an additional hole in the left-hand spindle fork to mount the new chainguard. This chainguard was hinged at the front, and independently bolted up at the rear. Previously, the lower rear suspension bolt had been used. At the same time, the chainguard was extended to cover more of the rear sprocket.

Forks A more rigid mounting for the front wheel spindle, in the form of split half clamps and $^5/_{16}$in bolts, was specified. The loose clips holding the front mudguard stays were dispensed with, and bottom members with induction brazed mounting lugs were fitted.

Petrol tank The new style 'mouth organ' tank badges and styling strips required a new petrol tank. The Triumph name was cast in the badge and inset white on a black background.

Oil tank No change.

Brakes The TR5 now featured a 7in diameter full width drum with a new spindle for the split fork ends. The TR6 featured the single sided 8in diameter brake with the alloy anchor plate with wire mesh air scoop. The wheel spindle was now the same as the TR5. The rear brake carried on as previously.

Wheels Both the TR5 and the TR6 came with the 19in diameter front rim fitted with either the 3.25 x 19 Dunlop ribbed or the 3.25 x 19 Dunlop Trials Universal.

The rear wheel remained as before, except that the 9 gauge spokes were replaced by the 8/10 gauge since the former were prone to breaking due to the extra power of the TR6. Rear tyres were Dunlop K70 4.00 x 18, Dunlop Trials Universal 4.00 x 18, or Dunlop Sports 4.00 x 18.

Mudguards No change except to finish.

Exhaust system No change.

Air filter No change.

Electrics From 04364 (1.1.1957), the TR6 was fitted with the Lucas Red Label magneto.

Speedo No change.

Tacho The Smiths RC1307/01 was an optional extra.

Handlebars No change.

Saddle No change.

Toolbox No change.

Extras
QD rear wheel	£3.14.5
Prop stand	£0.19.3
Pillion footrests	£0.19.11
Tacho kit	£7.15.10

Price
TR5	£257.18.5
TR6	£267.16.10

For the 1957 season there were a number of alternative

Technical development

TRIUMPH TROPHY 500/650 c.c.

TROPHY

The Triumph "Trophy" model, available with a choice of 500 c.c. or 650 c.c. engines, is a sporting mount with a world-wide reputation. In events where speed and stamina of the highest order are vital—like the I.S.D.T. in Europe and the big Enduros in U.S.A.—the "Trophy" has an enviable record, its reliability being almost legendary! It is easily adaptable to most forms of motorcycle sport and has a specification which includes all those features demanded by the sporting rider, features which have been tested and proved in active competition. "Trials" specification available for TR5 if required.

1957 Trophy.

specifications for the TR5:

TR5R
Twin carburettor splayed port alloy cylinder head fitted with racing interference valve springs (colour coded white), and bronze valve guides. High compression pistons giving 9.0:1 CR. Racing camshafts E3134 inlet and exhaust with E3059R $1^{1}/_{8}$ in radius followers. Carburettors were 376 Amal Monoblocs of 1in bore.

Engines with the above specification:
04638 - 16.1.1957, 010759 30.8.1957
08171 to 08181, 23.5.1957

TR5R
As above, but with the standard cylinder head fitted with twin Amal type 276 carburettors with remote float chamber.
04635 - 16.1.1957

04636 - 16.1.1957
04637 - 16.1.1957
05409 - 13.2.1957

TR5
Built as the TR5R but with standard single carburettor.
05882 - 26.2.1957
08182 to 08191 - 24.5.1957

TR5
Built 11.7.1957, 09554 to 09565 had E3275 ramp camshafts, 6.0:1 compression ratios, *etc.*, *i.e.* the same specification as the pre-1955 models.

A special TR5 was built with engine/frame number 06598 on 6th April 1957. The engine had special pistons giving a compression ratio of 5.0:1 and E3275 ramp camshafts were fitted to Speed Twin crankcases (no dynamo drive aperture). A Lucas race magneto supplied the ignition.

55

The Triumph Trophy Bible

TR5 Trophy built for the Swedish army. Note the 1957 petrol tank, but the 1956 forks and front wheel. The brackets on the front down tube and rear frame are for attaching skis.

When completed it was registered RWD 318 and was supplied to Artie Ratcliffe to ride in the 1957 Scottish Six Day Trial.

1958 TR5 and TR6 Trophy

Engine prefix: TR5 and TR6

Engine and frame numbers: 011861 to 019244
Build dates: 21.10.1957 to 25.6.1958

Engine The drive side crankcase was modified to accept an oil seal designed to eliminate oil transfer between the engine and primary cases, the engine sprocket boss was ground to suit.

Technical development

1958 Trophy TR6 with new fluted chromed cover on the front brake drum.

The TR6 featured a new cylinder head with reduced combustion spheres. The inlet valve head diameter was reduced to $1^{1}/_{2}$in from $1^{19}/_{32}$in, and the exhaust valve head diameter was reduced to $1^{11}/_{32}$in from $1^{7}/_{16}$in.

To counter cracking in the new reworked cylinder head, pistons with reshaped crowns were introduced at 012313 (4.11.1957).

Gearbox The gearbox featured the new 'Slickshift' mechanism, housed in the outer cover. Most noticeable was the repositioning of the clutch push rod operating lever, from the vertical to the horizontal position. Also, a chromed tin pressing covered the push rod adjuster screw. Although acclaimed by the Triumph advertising literature, it was not one of the company's best innovations, and it seemed the press of the day agreed, with comments like, "the revs had to be about right or there was a noticeable evidence of strain on the transmission", and, "unfortunately, the booted foot is less sensitive than the rider's hand". Fortunately, if the slickshift wasn't wanted, all one had to do was to cut off the roller arm from the footchange quadrant.

The other modifications to the gearbox were the introduction of a rubber sleeve between the kickstart lever and the gearbox case to aid oil retention, and the gearbox adjuster draw bolt now incorporated the clutch cable abutment.

Frame An anti-theft steering head lock was introduced, fitted on the right-hand side of the head lug casting. The primary chain adjuster draw bolt was modified to incorporate the clutch cable abutment.

Forks Brazed-on pommels for the centre mudguard stays were introduced on the inside of the fork member, giving a neater and cleaner appearance. The right-hand fork leg now incorporated the brake cable abutment with no adjuster at this point. A flanged steering stem nut was fitted to prevent the head lug creeping up the plain stem nut under extreme usage. The fork crown stem was slotted to accept the anti-theft steering lock.

Petrol tank No change.

Oil tank The filler cap was relocated, being moved further inboard so as not to foul the rider's leg when kickstarting.

Brakes The TR5 carried on as before, but the TR6 was fitted with a new 8in diameter full width front brake. Both brakes carried a fluted styling cover on the left side of the hub.

Wheels The TR6 8in full width hub was fitted with forty 8/10 gauge butted spokes.

Mudguards No change.

Exhaust system No change.

Air filter No change.

Electrics No change.

Speedo/tacho No change.

Seat No change.

Handlebars Although there was no change to the actual handlebar itself, both clutch and brake controls changed.

The Triumph Trophy Bible

Supplied in 500 c.c. or 650 c.c. form, the Triumph "Trophy" model is a tough, fast and durable mount for the competition rider. It has achieved successes without number throughout the world, and particularly in U.S.A., where, for example, in 1957, all three National Scrambles Championships were secured by "Trophy" riders. It can be readily adapted to most forms of motorcycle sport and will give complete satisfaction under the most arduous conditions.
Full Specification on pages 10/11.

1958 Trophy

The new controls were fitted with inbuilt cable adjusters and ball ends. Due to the lever brackets having no slotting, the cables were special and the cable nipples were loose slotted items.

Toolbox No change.

Extras
QD rear wheel	£3.14.11
Prop stand	£0.19.4
Pillion footrests	£1.00.0

Price
TR5	£274.9.0
TR6	£280.13.9

A twin carburettor conversion set was offered to fit the TR6, but only as an aftermarket accessory for dealer or owner fitment. The factory stressed a twin carb TR6 was not available ex-works.

1959 TR5 and TR6

Engine prefix: TR5 and TR6
Engine and frame numbers: 020883 to 029688
Build dates: 8.10.1958 to 10.9.1959

This was to be the last season for the Trophy TR5, as the 498cc 63 x 80mm engine was being discontinued across the range, with all future 500cc models having unit construction and 69 x 65.5mm engines.

As the TR6 was the pre-eminent Trophy by now, only two build batches of the TR5 were produced: 022269 to 022363 and 025724 to 025729, making a

Technical development

A twin high-level separate-pipe TR6, *circa* 1958, much liked in the USA.

The Triumph Trophy Bible

The 1959 TR6 could be finished in Ivory and Aztec Red livery, but only as an extra.

total for the season of 111.

Among this 111 total were a few choice Daytona specification models, 022278 to 022303 (7.11.1958 to 3.12.1958), and these were fitted with the following: twin carburettor splayed-port cylinder head; E3134 race camshafts with $1^{1}/_{8}$in radius cam followers; pistons with 9.0:1 compression ratio; interference race-type valve springs (white colour code); tachometer timing covers and tacho head; and finally, a Lucas K2FR racing magneto to provide the sparks.

022304 to 022340 were fitted with the same specification as above, but retained the standard TR5 single carburettor cylinder head.

025714 to 025726 were the standard TR5 Trophy, but were fitted with the E3134 race camshaft (inlet only), as well as a Lucas K2FR race magneto.

The last TR5 Trophy to be produced, number 025729, was built on 11th March 1959.

Engine The engine featured a forged one-piece crankshaft, with a bolt-on cast iron central flywheel held by three high tensile bolts. The essential crank dimensions remained as before, and the balance factor remained at 50%. A mid-season change was to increase the interference fit of the cast iron flywheel by 0.0025in, to overcome known retaining bolt failure. The TR6 E3325 inlet camshaft was replaced by a E3134 high performance race-type camshaft.

Gearbox An oil level indicator was built into the gearbox inner cover, and the oil level checked once the threaded plug was removed. The gear control camplate was induction hardened to improve long-term reliability.

Transmission No change.

Frame No change.

Forks No change.

Petrol tank No change.

Oil tank A froth tower was added to the oil tank to prevent oil loss when traversing rough terrain. The pipe from the tower still terminated into the rear of the primary chaincase.

Brakes The only change to the braking system was to the front brake cam lever, where the squared hole was repositioned to give a better angle. The reworked lever was identified by a letter X stamping.

Wheels No change.

Mudguards No change.

Exhaust system No change.

Air filter No change.

Electrical A new more robust voltage control box was fitted (Lucas 37725H) at 024824 (20.02.1959).

Speedo/tacho No change.

Handlebars No change.

Seat No change.

Toolbox No change.

Extras
QD rear wheel £3.14.11
Prop stand £0.19.4
Pillion footrests £1.0.0
Steering lock £0.13.2

Price TR6 £271.8.2

Technical development

1959 Trophy.

1959. A low-piped TR6 for the US market.

1960 TR6 Trophy TR6A and TR6B variants

Engine prefix: TR6
Engine and frame numbers: 029364 to 029688, then D904 to D6500

Build dates: 03.09.1959 to 29.06.1960

The TR6 took on a new look for this season, with a new frame featuring twin front down-tubes. The rear of the frame was bolted on as before.

The 1959 numbering system was initially carried

The TR5R was fitted with a splayed port cylinder head to take twin Amal Monoblocs.

over to the 1960 season's models until the prefix letter D was introduced.

Engine The crankcases were new to the TR6 for 1960, and the dynamo drive aperture was deleted. This modification harmonised the crankcases, as all models were now alternator-equipped. An alloy-bodied oil pump replaced the brass casting as a cost cutting measure.

Gearbox No change.

Transmission A 22 tooth engine sprocket replaced the earlier 24 tooth unit. This was necessary due to the adoption of a 43 tooth rear wheel sprocket.

Frame The new frame featured brazed lug construction, a single top tube, and twin front down tubes passing under the engine and gearbox. The rear frame was bolted to the front, as before, and supported Girling suspension units and the seat.

Forks The forks were redesigned to overcome spring friction, making them more responsive to minor irregularities. The internal springs were supported by guide tubes inside them, and two way oil damping was provided. The top and bottom yokes were also new, so as to be compatible with the new frame. As before, gaiters protected the sliding parts from dirt.

Petrol tank New for the 1960 season, and in both three and four gallon form, the petrol tank sat on three rubber buffers, and was held to the frame by a longitudinal, rubber lined, stainless steel strap. This was tensioned by a vertical threaded eye bolt at the head lug. Tank badges, luggage grid and knee grips remained as before.

Oil tank Of similar shape and capacity as before, the only differences being the fittings to the frame.

Brakes
Front - no change. Rear - the sprocket now carried 43 teeth, and was integral with the brake drum.

Wheels The only change was to the front wheel styling disc, the flutes were replaced by radial rings.

Mudguards The front guard changed to accommodate a new, neater, centre-mounting bridge. The front stay was redesigned to match.

Exhaust system No change.

Air filter No change.

Electrical The 7in chrome headlamp was only fitted with an ammeter, the light switch being positioned just below the seat nose on the right side. The Lucas 6 volt battery was charged by a crankshaft-driven alternator. The output of the alternator was converted to direct current via the Lucas FSX 1501A, $2^3/_4$in round, selenium plate rectifier. The ignition was still cared for by a Lucas K2FC magneto, with automatic ignition control for the USA, and manual control for Europe. A new Lucas 6SA D-shaped stop switch was specified.

Speedo
SC5301/09   140mph   1520rpm.
SC5301/16   190kph   950rpm.

Tacho No change.

Handlebars No change.

Seat A new seat to suit the redesigned rear frame. Seat trim was all black with grey piping.

Toolbox Similar to 1959 but with brackets to suit the new frame.

Variants
TR6A - A roadgoing model with Dunlop 3.25 x 19 ribbed front tyre and Dunlop K70 Universal 4.00 x 18

Technical development

TROPHY 650cc

Patent Nos. 475860, 474963, 482024

A sporting motorcycle of outstanding merit, the Trophy has a formidable record of success in all parts of the world and particularly in U.S.A., where the Jack Pine Enduro, Catalina Grand Prix, Big Bear Run (four years in succession) and most other American classics have been dominated by this model. Where the going is toughest, the Trophy is at its best!

"That's neat, an alternator for lighting in place of the separate dynamo."

(Below) Three studies of Bud Ekins, ace American rider, in action on his Triumph Trophy.

1960 Trophy.

rear. Two standard downswept exhaust pipes and two barrel-shaped silencers. Fitted with a tachometer driven from the timing cover.

TR6B - Fitted with 3.25 x 19 Dunlop Trials Universal on the front wheel, and 4.00 x 18 Dunlop Sports on the rear. Wide ratio gears were optional. The exhaust consisted of two high level pipes (one each side), fitted with leg guards with chevron piercing. The silencers were the small teardrop pattern.

Extras
QD wheel	£3.12.5
Prop stand	£0.18.9
Pillion footrests	£0.19.4
Steering lock	£0.12.8

Price £271.8.2

1961 TR6 Trophy TR6R and TR6C variants

Engine prefix: TR6, TR6R, TR6C
Engine and frame numbers: D8432 to D15756
Build dates: 20.9.1960 to 23.8.1961

The Trophy TR6 was not listed for sale in the UK this season.

Engine In the interests of quieter running, from D8858 the cylinder head had cast in pillars designed to prevent fin ring. The compression ratio was raised from 8.0:1 to 8.5:1.

From D14438, the crankshaft featured straight sided crank webs, and was fitted with a flywheel of increased width (to $2^{11}/_{32}$in from $2^{1}/_{4}$in). The balance

The Triumph Trophy Bible

The standard specification for a 1960 Trophy TR6C.

factor was increased to 71% by the use of 540 gram balance weights. The oil release valve pressure indicator shaft was fitted with an 'O' ring seal to overcome oil seepage in use.

Gearbox The sintered bronze layshaft bushes were

Technical development

Bird's-eye shot of the 1960 TR6C.

1960 TR6 seat, light switch and oil tank fittings.

replaced with Torrington M11121 $^{11}/_{16}$ x $^{7}/_{8}$ x $^{3}/_{4}$in needle roller bearings, with the layshaft modified to suit.

The primary chain adjuster was modified by moving the clutch cable abutment to the end of the draw bolt.

Transmission The engine sprocket was reduced by one tooth to 21, giving overall gear ratios of:

1st	11.92
2nd	8.25
3rd	5.81
4th	4.88

The Triumph Trophy Bible

This is a 1960 TR6A for Jo-Mo, USA.

Frame It was soon apparent that the new frame, introduced the previous year, was lacking in strength when used in the rough US enduro events. Breakages of the twin down tubes just under the steering head were not uncommon. This problem was completely eradicated by the inclusion of an additional lower tank rail. At the same time, the head

Technical development

A 1960 Trophy TR6B for TriCor, USA.

angle was changed from 67 degrees to 65 degrees.

Forks No change.

Petrol tank No change.

Oil tank No change.

Brakes Fully floating brake shoes were introduced, front and rear.

Wheels No change.

Mudguards No change.

Exhaust system No change.

Air filter No change.

The Triumph Trophy Bible

A Trophy TR6C of 1961. This is the one that everybody seems to like. The two colour paint scheme and twin high-level exhaust system give it character.

Electrical No change.

Speedo Smiths units as before, but revised due to the sprocket changes:
SC5301/26 mph (140mph)
SC 5301/18 kph (240kph)

Tacho No change.

Handlebars No change.

Seat No change.

Toolbox No change.

Extras
QD rear wheel	£4.2.10
Prop stand	£1.2.9
Pillion footrests	£1.2.1
Steering lock	£0.12.8
Tacho assembly	£9.2.10

Price £271.8.2

1962 TR6 S/S Trophy

Engine prefix: TR6 SS
Engine and frame numbers: D16189 to D20308
Build dates: 26.10.1961 to 31.07.1962

The TR6 S/S was the only Trophy produced for the 1962 season, becoming very much a single carburettor Bonneville.

Engine From D17043 (15.01.1962) the crankshaft balance factor was changed to 85%. This was to be the final figure and would remain so up to the introduction of the 750cc TR7. To accept the 85% factor a new pear-shaped crankshaft bobweight was required. At D17552 (19.02.1962), a cast iron oil pump body was fitted replacing the problematic alloy-bodied pump.

Gearbox The infamous 'slickshift' foot clutch control was quietly dropped for this season, with the only factory comment being, "It has outlived its usefulness".

Frame No change.

Forks No change.

Petrol tank New petrol taps with a spring loaded taper barrel retained by a circlip were fitted. This change was aimed at preventing jamming, something the previous taps were prone to.

Oil tank The oil tank was now fully rubber mounted, with a peg and rubber bush at the bottom fixing to eliminate cracking around the mounting brackets.

Brakes No change.

Wheels As before, but now shod with 3.25 x 19 Dunlop Ribbed on the front, and 4.00 x 18 Dunlop Universal K70 on the rear.

Mudguards No change.

Exhaust system New for 1962, the exhaust pipe was a siamezed low-level affair routed along the right side and terminating in a single barrel silencer.

Air filter No change.

Electrical A Lucas K2F magneto was now fitted, downgrading the specification, as the K2FC competition magneto was no longer thought necessary. A new fully waterproof metal-cased lighting switch with multi-pin socket and rubber cover was introduced.

At D18419 (15.03.1962), a new miniature rectifier (Lucas 49072 2DS506), was introduced, as was a Lucas 8H horn. The multi-pin QD socket was deleted from the headlamp shell after complaints of 'blackout' due to the plug and socket accidentally becoming detached.

Speedo/tacho No change.

Handlebars A flat sports-type handlebar bend was used for 1962, retaining the same controls and fittings as before.

Seat Although of the same shape and fitting as the previous year's seat, the cover changed for 1962, now having a grey top and lower trim band. Black sidewalls with white piping finished the seat off.

Toolbox No change.

Extras
QD rear wheel	£4.2.10
Prop stand	£1.2.9
Pillion footrests	£1.2.1
Steering lock	£0.15.4
Tacho assembly	£9.2.10

Price £280.19.1

The last pre-unit TR6 Trophy to be produced was D20308, on 30th July 1962.

1963 TR6 S/S

Engine prefix: TR6SS
Engine and frame numbers: DU102 to DU5790
Build dates: 29.09.1962 to 14.08.1963

For the 1963 season, an entirely new Trophy was introduced featuring unit construction of engine and gearbox. The new frame had a single front down tube, of $1\frac{3}{8}$in x 12G, with a strengthened swinging arm pivot tied up to the rear subframe via a hefty pivot lug.

Coil ignition was specified on the new engine, eliminating the long-established magneto ignition.

Engine A new crankcase assembly was fitted, incorporating the gearbox casing and primary drive. The cylinder barrel now featured nine cylinder head fixing bolts, with the $\frac{3}{8}$in ones being moved out radially to give more material between the bolt holes and the cylinder wall, and so eliminating bore distortion.

A new cylinder head, which accommodated the nine fixing bolts, also benefited from the relocated bolt

The Triumph Trophy Bible

A 1962 UK TR6.

Below: The 1962 TR6R, with low-level siamezed exhaust and optional tacho kit.

Technical development

"*A fast and rugged machine*" says BUD EKINS

—famous American cross-country star who has scored most of his innumerable successes in major U.S. events on Triumph Trophy models.

TROPHY 650 c.c. TR6S/S
Patent Nos. 475860, 469635, 684685

This fine sporting motorcycle is a firm favourite throughout the world and its specification includes every refinement demanded by the enthusiast. 40 B.H.P. engine, 2 into 1 exhaust, heavy duty competition type forks, duplex frame, rubber mounted fuel tanks and many other items which ensure success under the most arduous conditions.

holes which promoted reliability against cracking. New rocker boxes with horizontal finning, and new tappet inspection caps with serrated edges retained by locking clips, were also specified.

A new crankshaft featured an improved method of oil feed, via an oil seal in the timing cover, which replaced the bronze bush of the pre-unit model.

The exhaust camshaft was fitted with an internal taper to drive the Lucas contact breaker assembly housed in the timing cover. The timing pinions were increased in width to promote quieter operation.

Gearbox Integral with the engine and primary transmission, the layshaft continued to incorporate the speedo drive gear via the gearbox inner cover. A new gearbox outer cover incorporated a three ball clutch lift mechanism. Gears, shafts, *etc.,* remained as pre-unit.

Overall gear ratios altered slightly, to give 4.84, 5.76, 8.17, and 11.81, due to the new primary ratio.

Primary transmission Completely new primary transmission, comprising an 84 link duplex $^3/_8$in pitch chain with a cast iron clutch housing (58 teeth) and Langite cork friction pads. A duplex engine sprocket with 29 teeth completed the drive. An externally-adjustable blade-type tensioner was provided for primary chain adjustment.

The shock absorber unit was changed to a three paddle type, to give more movement, though this required new drive and rebound rubbers and a new pressure plate with three heavier springs replacing the previous four.

Frame The single front down tube frame carried a new swinging arm lug bolted up to the rear engine plates and

1962 Trophy.

the rear subframe. This, in conjunction with a new larger diameter tube swinging arm, gave very rigid mounting. An anti-theft lock and an easy-lift centre stand continued as standard equipment.

Forks No change.

Petrol tank A new three or four gallon tank, with two bolted rubber mountings at the front and one at the rear. Petrol taps, filler cap and parcel grid were as before, but the knee pads were changed to a stick-on pattern.

Oil tank The new oil tank was rubber-mounted, and had a capacity of six pints.

Side panel Opposite the oil tank was a side panel, covering the battery, and containing the ignition switch and the lighting switch.

Brakes As 1962.

Wheels As 1962, except that the rear wheel sprocket reverted to having 46 teeth (from 43 in previous years). This was due to the change in the primary drive ratio.

Mudguard Front - as 1962. Rear - new, to fit the redesigned frame and swinging arm.

Exhaust system The UK, Europe and general export models were fitted with siamezed low level pipes, on the right-hand side, with a single large silencer. US models, however, were fitted with twin low level exhaust pipes and barrel type silencers, if specified when ordered.

Air filter A round filter with a chromed perforated band was mounted directly onto the carburettor. To prevent the ingress of water, a metal shield was clipped onto the perforated band.

Electrical The Lucas 4CA contact breakers were housed in the timing cover, with the advance and retard mechanism being driven from the exhaust camshaft. Twin MA6 Lucas coils housed under the petrol tank provided the high tension voltage to the spark plugs.

The ignition switch and lighting switch were housed in the side panel on the left side of the machine. The chromed 7in Lucas headlamp was fitted with a 30/24 watt pre-focus bulb and a 2AR Lucas ammeter. The Lucas battery was a 6 volt amp/hour unit (MLZ9E 12). The Lucas 22B 31437 stop lamp switch was mounted on the rear chainguard. A spring and bracket attached to the brake rod provided the operation.

Speedo/tacho A Smiths chronometric speedo (SC53041/09 for mph, and SC5301/28 for kph) was now specified. Whilst the speedo was still driven from the gearbox layshaft, the tachometer (when fitted, since it was an optional extra), had a redesigned drive method. This took the form of an adapter threaded into the left-hand crankcase close to the end of the exhaust camshaft. The exhaust camshaft then drove a spindle within the adapter.

The cable screwed directly onto the adapter, forming a large loop before going up to the RC1307/01 chronometric tacho head.

Handlebars New $7/8$in diameter handlebars, to UK and US specification, were mounted via eye-bolts into anti-vibration metalastic bushes. Amal twistgrips replaced the Triumph units, and the clutch/brake levers continued with built-in cable adjusters (the brackets of which were now slotted for ease of assembly).

Seat Grey top with black side bands, and grey trim around the lower edge finished with white piping. The seat was now hinged to give access to the oil tank filler cap, battery and tool tray.

Toolbox A plastic tray bolted to the rear subframe.

Extras

QD rear wheel	£4.9.5
Prop stand	£1.4.8
Pillion footrests	£1.4.0
Steering lock	£0.16.3
Tacho assembly	£7.16.0

Price £303.0.0

1964 TR6 Trophy

Engine prefix: TR6SS, TR6R, TR6C, TR6SC, TR6SR
Engine and frame numbers: DU6127 to DU13287
Build dates: 29.08.1963 to 05.08.1964

Engine The engine breather pipe was extended to exit at the rear number plate, and linked to the oil tank breather via the froth tower. The carburettor size was increased too, the new specification being:

Amal Monobloc	389
Bore	$1^{1}/_{8}$in
Main jet	310
Needle jet	.106
Needle position	1
Needle type	D
Throttle valve	$3^{1}/_{2}$
Pilot jet	25

Gearbox An oil seal was fitted in the gearbox outer cover to prevent oil seepage along the kickstart spindle.

Transmission From DU7036 (04.11.1963), anti-rotational spring cups were fitted to the clutch pressure plate. The engine sprocket on the C models was modified to accept a dowel peg for rotor timing, giving greater accuracy for the Energy Transfer ignition system.

Frame Redesigned footrests now mounted directly onto the rear engine plates to improve ground clearance. The centre stand operating arm was brazed-in, making it integral with the stand, replacing the earlier cottered one.

Forks A new fork assembly was featured for the 1964 season. For the first time in Triumph's telefork history,

Technical development

external fork springs were employed. A chrome plated lower spring carrier housed a double lipped oil seal. Rubber gaiters covered the springs and prevented dirt ingress. A rubber bush was interposed between the steering damper rod and the hollow tube of the steering stem to prevent rotation due to vibration.

The C models were fitted with a fork top lug with rigid handlebar mountings, similar to the pre-1963 pattern. The amount of oil was amended to $\frac{1}{3}$ pint (200cc) of SAE 20 for each leg.

Petrol tank No change.

Oil tank The engine breather pipe was routed up to the oil tank and connected to the oil tank breather pipe via a cranked T piece. It was then routed along the rear mudguard, and terminated below the number plate.

Brakes No change.

Wheels No change.

Mudguards A new front mudguard was required to accommodate the new tubular middle stay. Loose pear-shaped mounting plates were used to attach the front and centre stays.

Exhaust No change.

Air filter No change.

Electrical A Lucas 8H horn was fitted to give a louder note. The TR6C and SC were fitted with the new Energy Transfer batteryless ignition/lighting system. Also, on the TR6C and SC, the alternator rotor was timed to the engine sprocket by a dowel rather than the normal crankshaft keyway and key.

Speedo/tacho The new Smiths magnetic anti-vibration instruments were fitted, speedo SSM5 001/00 replaced SC 5301/09; tachometer RSM 3001/02 replaced RC 1307/01, when specified.

Handlebar No change.

Seat No change.

Toolbox No change.

Extras
QD rear wheel	£4.9.5
Prop stand	£1.4.8
Pillion footrests	£1.4.0
Steering lock	£0.16.3
Tacho	£7.16.0

Price £307.4.0

1965 TR6 Trophy TR6SS, TR6SR, TR6SC, TR6

Engine prefix: TR6, TR6SS, TR6SR, TR6SC

This shot of the under seat area of the TR6 shows the oil tank/engine breather pipes, and the position of the oil recommendation transfer.

The Trophy TR6SC 'Desert Sled'. Polished alloy mudguards, direct battery-less ignition and straight-through exhaust were features on this 1964 model.

Engine and frame numbers: DU14226 to DU23732
Build dates: 27.8.1964 to 21.6.1965

Engine For this year only, the crankshaft end float was controlled by the drive side main bearing via the engine sprocket. The crankshaft flywheel now featured a location slot enabling the engine to be locked at TDC through the crankcase timing plug situated at the rear of the cylinder barrel.

The oil pressure relief valve was fitted with a plain dome nut, deleting the oil pressure telltale indicator button.

Gearbox The kickstart ratchet pinion sleeve was fitted with a washer to ensure a more positive location between the sleeve and the bearing. The splines on the high gear and gearbox sprocket altered too. Note: Individual components are not interchangeable, they can only be fitted as a set.

Transmission A longer alternator cable sleeve nut was fitted to stop the cable being fouled by the primary chain.

Frame The swinging arm pivot bolt thread location was relocated to the left side to improve accessibility. A revised horn mounting bracket was welded to the lower tank rail.

The rear brake pedal was redesigned to give a straight pull for the brake rod, with the brake pedal pivot spindle operating through the bushed engine plate.

The centre stand was fitted with new pivot bolts with lock tabs, preventing the nuts loosening in use.

Forks The fork travel was increased by 1in by fitting shorter bottom sliders, longer $9^3/_4$in springs, and 22in stanchions. The alloy damper sleeve was redesigned to have only one stepped end to aid assembly.

Petrol tank No change.

Oil tank No change.

Brakes No change.

Wheels No change to front. Rear QD - taper roller bearings in the hub were deleted, and replaced with LS8-V3 ball journal bearings ($^3/_4$ x $1^7/_8$ x $^9/_{16}$in). This modification meant a redesigned rear hub and spacer tubes.

Mudguards No change.

Exhaust No change.

Air filter No change.

Electrical The Lucas 8H horn was relocated to face sideways on the lower tank rail under the fuel tank. The US models were fitted with a new Lucas tail lamp, type 679, commonly known as the teat type.

Speedo/tacho No change.

Handlebars Slight modifications to the actual bend which the factory claimed "gave a more comfortable riding position" were fitted.

Seat No change.

Toolbox No change.

Extras
QD rear wheel	£4.14.1
Prop stand	£1.6.0
Pillion footrests	£1.5.1
Steering lock	£0.17.1
Tacho	£8.3.8
Price	£320.13.10

1966 TR6

Engine prefix: TR6, TR6R, TR6SR, TR6SS, TR6C, TR6SC
Engine and frame numbers: DU24876 to DU43161
Build dates: 6.8.1965 to 8.7.1966

Engine The cylinder head was fitted with 'red spot' valve springs, with the following dimensions:

Number of coils	$5^1/_2$
Free length outer	$1^5/_8$in
Free length inner	$1^{17}/_{32}$in
Fitted length outer (inlet)	$1^7/_{32}$in
Fitted length inner (inlet)	$1^3/_{16}$in
Fitted length outer (exhaust)	$1^5/_{32}$in
Fitted length inner (exhaust)	$1^1/_8$in
Fitted load-valve closed	50lb

With the new shorter spring, a thicker bottom spring cup was called for. This modification ensured better valve control with less spring surge.

A new flywheel, with a reduced weight of $2^1/_2$lb, was fitted to the crankshaft. To maintain the 85% balance factor, the periphery of the flywheel was stepped in cross section. The crankshaft end float control reverted to the right side mainbearing, via a clamping washer interposed between the timing pinion and the mainbearing inner spool. A heavier, load carrying single lipped roller bearing (RM11L), replaced the ball journal bearing on the drive side.

Pressure feed to the exhaust cam followers was introduced, feeding through drillways in the crankcase and cylinder barrel to the exhaust tappet block. At DU42399, 29.6.1966, a dowel was introduced between the crankcase and cylinder barrel joint to overcome oil seepage.

Redesigned straight-walled push rod cover tubes were flanged top and bottom. The bottom sealing washer was retained in a cupped washer fitted over the tappet block. Redesigned tappet guide blocks were also specified to accept the new cover tubes.

From DU42251, $1^1/_8$in radius 'R' type cam followers replaced the $^3/_4$in radius ones. The inlet valve head diameter was increased to $1^{19}/_{32}$in, and the exhaust to $1^7/_{16}$in, to harmonise with the Bonneville T120.

Technical development

The standard 1965 season Trophy TR6 for the UK.

A 1965 Trophy TR6R for the US market, fitted with a tacho and extended rear lamp carrier.

Gearbox The layshaft speedometer drive gear was deleted, as were the inner cover bush and driven gear. The kickstart lever was redesigned, and given a longer lever to ease starting.
Specified sprockets for 1966 were as follows:

TR6, TR6R, TR6SS, TR6SR	19 tooth
TR6C	18 tooth
TR6SC	17 tooth

Transmission The pressure plate adjusting screw diameter was increased to $^3/_8$in from DU31820 (18.12.1965). The rear chain oiler in the rear of the primary case was discontinued.

Frame The frame steering head angle was changed from 65 to 62 degrees, and, at the same time, fairing lugs were added to the head lug forging. A new rear frame was specified for 1966, with welded pegs to mount new

The Triumph Trophy Bible

A Jomo TR6SC. This model features Dunlop Universal Trials tyres and twin high-level exhaust.

battery carrier mounting cross-straps. These new battery carrier straps had tubular ends to accept spiggoted rubber bushes.

A new switch panel was now mounted to the cross-straps, and carried the new Yale-type barrel ignition switch and the lighting switch.

A new swinging arm was specified which had the right-hand fork moved out by $1/4$in, from $3^1/_2$ to $3^3/_4$in. A central line, therefore, drawn through the swinging arm would show $3^1/_2$in on the left side and $3^3/_4$in on the right.

The TR6SC was fitted with folding footrests to comply with AMA regulations.

Forks A new fork stem and bottom lug was used to give a tighter turning circle. The damper spacer sleeves changed from aluminium to plastic, but retained the same dimensions from DU31820 (18.12.1965).

Petrol tank The new tank was slimmer, available in 3 or 4 gallon capacity, and came with the new design of tank

Technical development

The 1966 TR6C was aimed specifically at the American market. The cast alloy rear lamp housing, white rubber handlebar grips, and 'eyebrow' tank badge were new for 1966.

badge commonly known as the eyebrow badge. Fittings continued as 1963.

Oil tank The new oil tank had provision for rear chain oiling via an adjustable metering screw in the filler cap neck. Also, the rocker feed was taken from the top of the return pipe rather than below the tank. (This alteration was not successful, however, and would cause premature rocker wear. A service kit to reverse this was offered).

Brakes A new front brake drum and wider brake shoes provided a 40% increase in braking area.

Wheels The rear wheel sprocket reverted to the 46 teeth bolt-on type. The QD wheel retained the cast integral sprocket. Both rear hubs were now threaded internally to take a slotted sleeve to drive the Smiths speedo gearbox.

Mudguards No change.

Exhaust system No change.

Air filter No change.

Electrical Apart from the TR6C, all were fitted with a 12 volt zener diode-controlled system. Up to DU32895 (6.1.1966), two Lucas MKZ9E batteries were fitted. Thereafter, a single Lucas PUZ5A battery, which required a modified battery carrier, was specified. The 7in chrome headlamp incorporated both ignition warning and headlamp main beam warning lights (after DU29247). The ignition coils were Lucas MA12, still located as before, but some US models were fitted with the smaller Siba 3200/1 ignition coil. The Lucas 88SA multi-pin light switch remained in the left-hand side panel, as did the new ignition switch, now having a Yale-type key and barrel lock.

The zener diode was mounted on a flat aluminium plate bolted to the battery carrier. However, due to overheating problems, a larger plate with a right angle extension was fitted after DU40436 (2.5.1966).

The US models featured a polished alloy casting to carry the Lucas 679 tail light.

Speedo A Smiths SSM 5001/00A speedometer was now specified. A longer cable was required to reach the rear wheel driven speedo gearbox (also a Smiths unit: BG 5330/287 with a 2.0:1 ratio).

Tacho A new tachometer instrument, Smiths RSM 3003/01A, was specified to ensure compatibility with the new right angle drive tacho gearbox. A new shorter drive cable was also called for.

Handlebars White rubber handlebar grips were fitted, for this season only.

Seat No change.

Toolbox No change.

Extras
  Tachometer   £9.0.3d
  QD rear wheel   £5.3.9d

The Triumph Trophy Bible

1966 Triumph brochure.

The ultimate in rugged, sporting motorcycles, with all the power and stamina needed to win major events, regardless of conditions, the Trophy has earned an unrivalled, world-wide reputation for sheer performance and staying power. Consistent winner of gold medals in the International Six Days' Trial and successes in the toughest of American enduros, this machine's breathtaking acceleration and superb roadholding characteristics provide even the most experienced sportsman with the supreme satisfaction of an exhilarating ride.

Prop stand	£1.8.9d
Pillion footrests	£1.7.6d
Steering lock	£0.18.10d

Price £336.16.4

Variations

TR6C: Basically the same specification as the TR6 but with the following essential differences:

Gearbox: Wide ratio gears unless otherwise specified at point of order.

Petrol tank: A slimmer tank, of 2.3 gallon capacity, was fitted as standard.

Tyres: Usually a 3.25 x 19 Dunlop Trials Universal was fitted to the front wheel, whilst the rear was a 4.00 x 18 Dunlop Trials Universal or a Dunlop Sports.

Exhaust system: Two high level pipes running over the primary chaincase terminating into two small round barrel silencers. Leg guards were fitted to the exhaust pipes.

Electrical: A 6in diameter Lucas headlamp was fitted. This had a black painted shell which housed the headlight dip push switch and the rotary on off light switch. Ignition was the Energy Transfer type, and direct lighting was fed by the alternator. A Lucas push switch was handlebar-mounted to provide the ignition cut-out.

TR6SC: As TR6C, but with the following differences:

Gearbox: Standard ratio gears.

Mudguards: Aluminium alloy.

Exhaust: As TR6C, but straight through extensions

Technical development

1966 model Trophy TR6SR for the USA.

replaced the silencers.

Electrical: Only the ignition system was fitted and, as with the TR6C, this was the Energy Transfer type. The SC was only built for the US and was designed for desert racing, with most of the output going to Jomo on the West Coast. Price was around $1200.

TR6SR: Basically, a standard TR6, but with raised handlebars and a smaller capacity petrol tank.

1967 TR6 Trophy

Engine prefix: TR6, TR6R, TR6C, TR6P
Engine and frame numbers: DU46201 to DU66246
Build dates: 14.9.1966 to 3.7.1967

Engine Hepworth and Grandage-manufactured pistons replaced the Triumph components, though the 9.0:1 compression ratio was retained. The following may help with identification:

Crown height from gudgeon pin centre:

Comp. ratio	Crown height
11.0:1	1.845/1.849in
9.0:1	1.498/1.502in
8.5:1	1.488/1.492in
7.5:1	1.416/1.424in

From DU63043 (1.5.1967), the final form of exhaust camshaft oiling was introduced, in the form of timed tappets. Full oil pressure was fed to the exhaust tappet block and then to the cam lobes via the tappets, which had timed ports so that oil was only supplied as the cam raised the tappet.

'O' ring seals were fitted to the tappet guide blocks from DU63241, to prevent oil seepage between tappet block and barrel.

The oil pump, with increased scavenge capacity, was fitted to maintain the desired level in the crankcase.

From DU63043, the Amal Monobloc carburettor was replaced by the Amal Concentric, with the following specifications:

Amal Concentric	R930/9-B
Bore	30mm

79

The Triumph Trophy Bible

This 1966 TR6P Saint (stop anything in no time), is shown in Metropolitan Police specification. Note the Queen's Award to Industry badge on the side panel.

Main jet	230
Valve cutaway	3½
Needle	622/124
Needle position	2
Needle jet	.106
Spray tube	622/074

Gearbox A new gearbox mainshaft, with a lengthened thread at the end, allowed the use of a self lock nut and plain washer, replacing the stepped nut and tab washer. This was fitted from DU54659 (28.12.1966). From DU64758 (18.05.1967), alternate engagement dogs on the mainshaft second gear were deleted to aid gear selection.

Transmission The clutch hub extractor thread was changed from CEI to UNF from DU54659 (28.12.1966).

Frame The anti-theft lock barrel housing was deleted from the midway point of the steering head lug. Threaded steering stop pegs were introduced at the lower end of the head lug. At the top of the steering head lug, the left side accommodated the peg of the anti-theft steering lock. Threaded items within the frame now carried UNF threads.

Forks A new fork top lug, designed to accept the Yale-type anti-theft lock, was specified. The fork spring gaiters now featured wire spring clips replacing the worm and strap as before.
From DU54659, 'O' ring seals were added to the fork seal holders to prevent oil seepage. To accommodate

Technical development

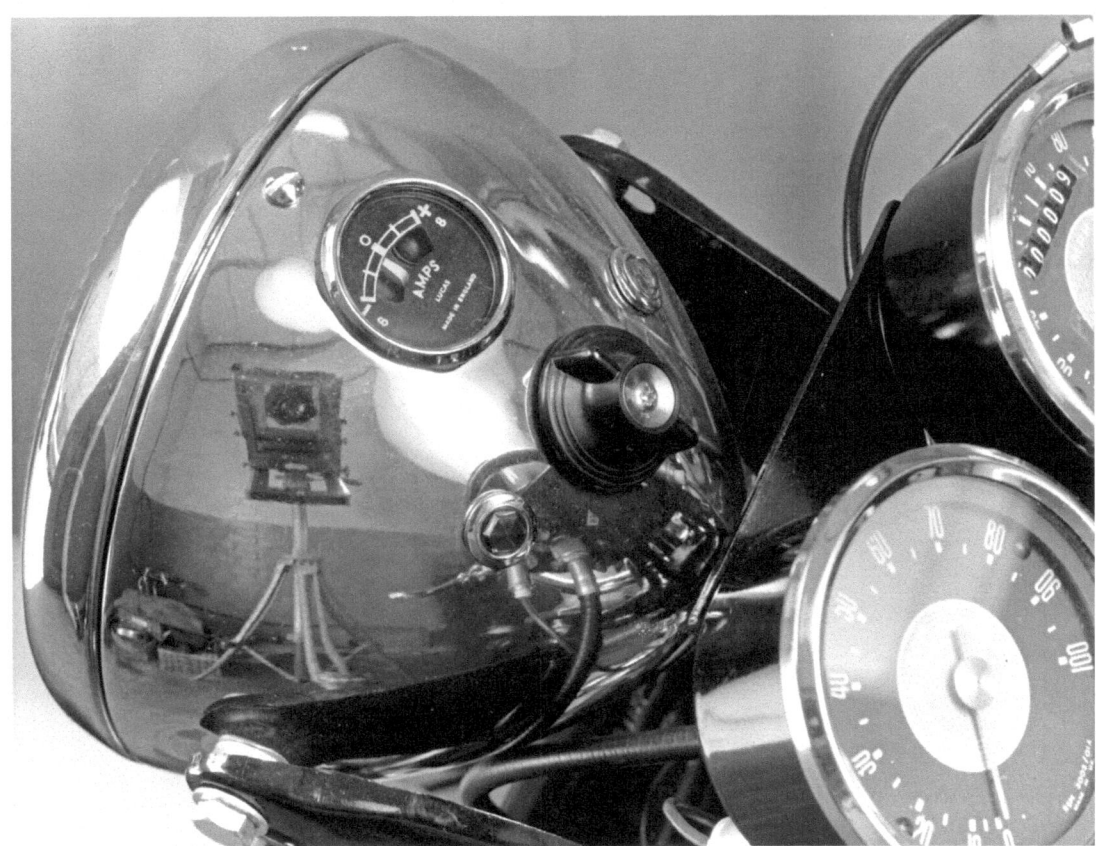

The 1967 TR6 was fitted with a rotary light switch and eight amp ammeter, whereas the 1968 model had a lever switch and a twelve amp ammeter. Note also the differing locations of the warning lights.

the 'O' ring, the first two threads were removed from the bottom members.

Petrol tank The luggage grids were no longer fitted to the US models, so the threaded pommels were deleted from the tank top.

Oil tank From DU54659, the rocker feed reverted to the 1965 arrangement, where the take-off pipe was below the oil tank.

Brakes No change.

Wheels All models now featured a 19in diameter front wheel. Non US models were fitted with ribbed 3.25 x 19 Dunlops on the front, and 3.50 x 18 K70s on the rear.

Mudguards No change.

Exhaust system On the downswept exhaust system, two short angle brackets were fitted, tying each pipe to the crankcase mounting stud.

Air filter No change.

Electrical From DU58993, the Lucas two-lead stator was encapsulated completely, so avoiding the problem of failure due to coils shorting out. From DU54659, the auto advance cam was changed to 160 degrees dwell to prevent the idle spark causing piston failure. A louder Lucas 6H horn was fitted.

Speedo No change.

Tacho A 'Stat-o-Seal' washer was fitted between the tachometer gearbox face and the crankcase to prevent oil seepage.

Handlebars Those models fitted with raised US handlebars, were fitted with extra rubber washers and metal cups to prevent the fore and aft rocking movement of the bars.

The 1966 white handlebar grips were replaced by black Gran-Turisimo ones, of Italian manufacture.

Seat A new grey quilted top with white piping, black sidewalks, and grey lower trim band. The rear of the seat had a distinct upward tilt. The seat catch plunger now had an integral black plastic knob replacing the previous detachable chrome knob.

Toolbox No change.

Extras
Tachometer	£9.6.0
QD rear wheel	£5.5.6
Prop stand	£1.9.0
Pillion footrests	£1.7.6
Steering lock	£0.19.6

Price £342.0.0

1968 TR6

Engine prefix: TR6, TR6R, TR6C, TR6P
Engine and frame numbers: DU68364 to DU85903
Build dates: 9.8.1967 to 26.6.1968

Engine The exhaust camshaft was replaced with the race type E3134, making inlet and exhaust cams the same, and harmonising the Trophy with the Bonneville. $1^1/_8$in radius followers continued to be specified for both inlet and exhaust.

The outer valve springs were modified (identified by green paint), to give 10% increased load when the valve was fully open, but retaining the original loading when closed.

Spring dimensions:
Free length outer	$1^1/_2$in
Number of coils	$5^3/_4$
Fitted load with valve closed	75lbs

From DU81209 (15.03.1968), the oilways through the rocker arms were deleted, the rocker arms gaining additional strength to cope with the new valve springs.

Stronger connecting rods were specified. 1 inch below the small end now measured 0.650in in thickness, whereas the previous rods measured 0.550in. The H & G pistons were redesigned, with the bar under the piston crown being removed, and the area around the ring grooves thickened to prevent distortion. Problems of the tachometer gearbox loosening off in use were rectified by changing the fixing bolt to left-hand thread.

To gain adequate spanner access, the cylinder barrel retaining nuts were changed to the 12 point type.

For 1968, there were three conditions of crankcase/flywheel providing TDC, or 38 degrees BTDC.

MkI. The timing plug was situated at the lower front of the crankcase, and there was one hole or slot in the flywheel below the crank bobweight. This condition gave 38 degrees BTDC only.

MkII. Two timing plugs were fitted to the crankcase, one as MkI and the other behind the cylinder barrel. The flywheel holes or slots were situated with one below the bobweight and one above, giving 38 degrees BTDC and TDC.

MkIII. The timing plug for the final condition was behind the cylinder barrel, and the flywheel had two slots situated above the crankpin, giving both 38 degrees BTDC and TDC. This final condition was fitted from DU74052 (6.11.1967).

Gearbox The mainshaft high gear was extended to fully envelop the bush, the oil seal now bearing directly on the steel gear. This modification called for a revised oil seal and primary cover plate. The gearbox mainshaft was modified to provide UNF threads at both ends. The clutch operating mechanism was modified, with the spoke and cable anchorage thimble now deleted. The new system ran the cable directly onto the new lifting arm lever. The cable and gearbox outer cover were also new, with the latter requiring a threaded inspection plug adjacent to the cable nipple attachment. The camplate plunger housing was changed to UNC thread, identifiable by being a full hexagon for its total length.

The traditional Triumph gear pedal rubber lost the Triumph logo, and was replaced by a BSA Bantam type. Also receiving the same treatment was the kickstart rubber, which now had a through hole replacing the closed end logo-styled rubber.

Transmission The primary outer cover was fitted with a detachable circular cover, so that ignition timing, via scribed lines on the rotor, could be accurately set.

Technical development

A nice factory photo of a 1968 US TR6R. Riviera Blue and Silver Sheen gave it a bright look.

At DU85346 (19.06.1968), to further aid the timing procedure, a fixed pointer was added to the primary cover.

Frame A modified front frame, with the head lug incorporating an extended lock shelf to prevent accidental lock peg engagement, was specified. The rear frame was also modified to provide locating pegs on the left down tube to secure the new detachable side panel which incorporated the toolbox.

A stronger swinging arm with heavier corner fillets and heavier gauge tube (14G to 12G), was used from DU81209 (15.03.1968). Identification for the revised swinging arm was by a letter 'X' stamped into the pivot tube. To aid lubrication, a $1/16$in hole was added to the pivot tube seal covers to provide venting. An entirely new prop stand, consisting of a one piece forging with a long curved arm, was fitted.

Forks A new fork assembly housed the ignition switch

The Triumph Trophy Bible

The Trophy TR6C of 1968 featured stainless steel mudguards, twin high-level exhaust and a twin leading shoe front brake.

in the left-hand top cover, the bottom lug carried a threaded boss to mount the zener diode heat sink. Most importantly, from the handling point of view, was the introduction of the shuttle valve damping which gave more controlled movement.

Some of the early season's models were fitted with sintered iron fork bushes, but problems in use meant a swift reversion to the sintered bronze type. Finally, from DU68364, the threads on the fork assembly changed from CEI to UNF.

Petrol tank US models had reflector mounting pods attached by the front tank bolts. After DU81209, the front tank mounting bolts were replaced by studs and nuts. 'Stat-O-Seal' washers were fitted between the petrol tap locking nuts and the tank to prevent seepage.

Oil tank No change.

Technical development

Brakes A new 8in front brake with twin leading shoes and an air scoop anchor plate was fitted. From DU70083, a split pin was fitted to the anchor plate brake cable abutment for safety reasons.

Wheels A longer front wheel spindle was fitted to accept the new front brake. The brake drum styling plate was redesigned, fluted, and was larger than the actual brake drum. It was retained by three small screws.

Mudguards The front mudguard was lengthened slightly from DU81709, but not on the TR6C.

Exhaust From DU82574 (1.4.1968), the TR6C upswept pipes were coupled by a separate 'H' piece before entering the silencers. This modification was brought about by the impending noise regulations.

Air filter No change.

Electrical The zener diode was relocated to the front fork middle lug, and housed in a finned heat sink. The new headlamp shell now housed a three position lighting switch, along with a more robust Lucas ammeter and high beam/ignition warning lights.

The barrel-type ignition switch continued as 1967, but was now relocated to the left-hand fork cover. A new Lucas 6CA contact breaker assembly featured independently positioned and adjustable contact points. To make room for this assembly, the condensers were repositioned to the front petrol tank mounting bracket, taking the form of a twin pack fitted with a moulded rubber cover. At DU82146, lubricating felt wicks were added to the contact assembly, to combat premature wear of the contact breaker heels. All models were fitted with a deeper pressing points cover to house the 6CA contact assembly.

The new alternator rotor had cast in raised areas, on which was a scribed line. When this line and primary case pointer aligned, 38 degrees BTDC was indicated.

The TR6C was fitted with a $5^3/_4$in diameter headlamp, now chrome plated, which kept the ignition warning light in the centre, the push rotary dip switch on the right, and the pilot-main selection rotary switch on the left. The ignition continued as before with the Energy Transfer system.

The US models were fitted with the Lucas 679 teat-type tail lamp, though now fitted to a new polished alloy housing with triangular reflectors on each side.

Clearhooter horns replaced the Lucas ones.

Speedo/tacho No change.

Handlebars No change.

Seat A new twinseat, with external hinges made from pressings, replaced the previous seat and forged J-shaped hinges. The new seat had a grey ribbed top, white piping, black sidewalks, and a chromed plastic beading around the lower edge. The seat pan also incorporated threaded bosses to take a passenger grab rail. This grab rail was only fitted as standard to US models.

Toolbox The toolbox was incorporated in the detachable left-hand side panel. This side panel was retained by a plastic knob secured by a click spring to prevent accidental unscrewing and loss of the panel.

Note: Starting with the 1968 season models, a process of changing all the threaded components from CEI to UNF and UNC started. As all the items/components could not be changed at once, it means that a mixture of threads can be found on any 1968 and 1969 models. In general terms, one finds that the CEI threads up to $7/_{16}$in diameter had 26TPI, whereas the UNF threads were:

28TPI for $1/_4$in diameter
24TPI for $5/_{16}$in diameter
24 TPI for $3/_8$in diameter

A close-up of the new-for-'68 front brake and cable routing.

The Triumph Trophy Bible

20 TPI for 7/16in diameter
20 TPI for 1/2in diameter

Extras

Tachometer	£9.6.0
QD rear wheel	£5.5.6
Prop stand	£1.9.0
Pillion footrests	£1.7.6
Steering lock	£0.19.6

Price £342.6.0

1969 Model Tiger TR6

Engine prefix: TR6, TR6R, TR6C, TR6P
Engine and frame numbers: DU87124 to DU88524 then NC02352 to HC2434
Build dates: 29.7.1968 to 14.8.1968, then 26.10.1968 to 15.7.1969

1969 was notable for the demise of the Trophy name in the sales brochures. The TR6 was given the more fashionable name of Tiger. It seems that this didn't register with the factory workers, though, as they carried on referring to the TR6 as a Trophy for many years.

The 1969 season saw the end of the DU engine/frame number prefix, which had been used since 1963. Henceforth, a two or three letter prefix would be used to indicate the month and year of manufacture. The engine number was also stamped onto a raised pad, into which the Triumph logo was impressed. This served to aid in the identification of stolen motorcycles.

The threads in the crankcase halves, gearbox casings and primary cases all changed to UNF and UNC.

The oil pump feed plunger was increased in diameter, as was the pump body, increasing the volume of oil delivered. From NC02352 (26.10.1968), the crankcase scavenge tube was shortened to $1^{13}/_{16}$in, allowing more oil to remain in the crankcase. The crankshaft flywheel weight was increased, though the 85% balance factor was retained.

New connecting rods were specified which, although they retained the same dimensions, had UNF bolts and self-lock nuts. The torque figure changed from 28 to 22lbft.

Hepolite pistons with a thicker crown and shorter, thicker gudgeon pin, were also specified.

To improve long term reliability, and to put a complete end to camshaft wear problems, a nitriding process was introduced for the camshafts.

Push rod covers/tubes were redesigned once again. Viton 'O' ring seals top and bottom maintained a diametrical sliding fit over the tappet guide block and in the cylinder head counterbore. In the never-ending quest for oil tightness, the chaincase and gearbox filler caps were fitted with 'O' ring seals from HC23617 (8.7.1969), replacing the fibre washers.

The alternator cable outlet was repositioned to exit from the top of the chaincase, rather than near the gearbox sprocket, overcoming the problem of the cable and chain fouling.

To prevent internal frothing, the Amal Concentric carburettor was given an anti-vibration mounting. This modification required a new manifold, manifold studs, and carburettor flange 'O' ring seal.

Gearbox The gearbox camplate was improved by the use of a precision pressing during manufacture. This gave a much better finish to both the outer periphery and the inner cam tracks. The gears were treated to a 'shaving' process which improved the finish, thereby reducing noise and wear when in use. Unfortunately, a decision taken outside the company's jurisdiction slightly changed all the gear shaft spline and gear bore diameters, enough to ensure non-interchangeability with the earlier ones. This modification came into effect from CC15546 (15.4.1969).

A change to the third gear ratio, whereby 22/23 tooth gears replaced 22/24, had the effect of lowering the third gear internal ratio, down from 1.19 to 1.14.

Transmission The clutch sprocket housing's cast-in pockets were deleted, with the sprocket drum now fully machined on its periphery. This modification removed any imbalance that could arise. From HC23617, (8.7.1969), the location ears on the clutch thrust washer were deleted, as were (eventually) the two location holes in the clutch hub.

Frame From HC23617, the prop stand was fitted with an adjustable stop bolt to prevent the stand crashing into the exhaust. The Girling suspension units lost the tin covers, and now had exposed chromed springs.

Forks The redesigned top lug, fork crown and stem increased the stanchion tube centres to $6^3/_4$in (previously $6^1/_2$in), giving more mudguard/tyre clearance. From BC12825 (25.2.1969), modified fork stanchions with added bleed holes, $5/_{64}$in diameter, 1 and 2 inches from the lower bush shoulder, improved the damping. The steering stem nut was now a domed chrome component, with the steering damper knob and assembly being deleted on all models except the C. A grommet was introduced into the right-hand headlamp bracket to take the throttle cable, and tidy up the run of the cable.

Petrol tank The new style tank badge with altered fixing holes meant a new range of tanks to suit. The new badge had the Triumph motif within a square framed border. The chromed centre styling band was now retained by a threaded hook through the rear tank fixing bracket. The tank parcel grid was removed from the US specification due to fears of more compensation claims (a Triumph mounted rider was involved in an accident and, in the ensuing *melee*, the unfortunate rider caught his testicles on the grid. The resulting court case cost Triumph a lot of money).

Oil tank No change to the actual tank, but the filler cap was fitted with a dip stick level gauge.

Brakes The front brake anchor plate was modified to give a vertical cable run, the brake cam lever being modified to suit. This improved the previous cable run which had

Technical development

A new four gallon petrol tank, with new bird wing badges, graced the 1968 UK Trophy TR6, as shown on this 1969 model. The tyre inflator was only fitted to UK models.

looped alongside the mudguard and had proved vulnerable to damage. A brake light stop switch was incorporated in the front brake cable.

Wheels The front wheel was fitted with a longer spindle to suit the wider fork centres. A new concentrically ribbed front hub cover plate was also fitted.

Mudguards No change.

Exhaust To combat the growing noise level demands, a coupling pipe was introduced into the down pipes, near the cylinder head, and all twin downswept systems were fitted with the US type silencer. The TR6C, with its upswept pipes, continued with the two pipes linked by a 'H' piece. The silencers were now the larger-bodied US ones, with a large wire mesh leg guard, often referred to as the 'chip basket'.

Air filter No change.

Electrical A Smiths oil pressure switch was introduced. This fitted to the front of the timing cover and operated a red warning light in the headlamp shell. A brake light stop switch was located between the two sections of the front brake outer casing. Compression of the outer during braking activated the electrical contacts in the switch. The US models were fitted with SIBA ignition coils, whilst the rest continued with the Lucas components. The Lucas 679 tail lamp, previously only for the US, became a standard fitting for all models.

Speedo The Smiths speedometer for the 1969 season was SSM 5501/06. The rear wheel gearbox was BG 5330/168, with a 1.25:1 ratio.

Tacho No change.

Handlebars From NC02352, on all models except the C, the handlebar eye bolts were fitted with extra rubber washers and keeper cups to prevent any possibility of contact between the eye bolt and the frame head lug. Ball ended levers became standard on all models.

Seat No change.

Toolbox No change.

Rear number plate - UK A new pressing was required to accommodate the Lucas 679 rear light.

Extras
  Tachometer   £10.4.0
  QD rear wheel   £6.10.9

Price £369.19.11

1970 TR6 Tiger

Engine prefix: TR6, TR6R, TR6C, TR6P

The Triumph Trophy Bible

The TR6C sported a 'go-faster' stripe and Trophy 650 motif for 1969. The 'rigid' handlebar mounting was standard on the TR6C.

Engine and frame numbers: HD23795 to ND60540
Build dates: 9.7.1969 to 8.10.1970

Engine Both inlet and exhaust camshaft threads were changed to UNF, and breather holes in the inlet camshaft were deleted, as was the rotary breather valve. The tacho drive pressed steel thimble in the exhaust camshaft was replaced by a slotted threaded plug. From PD32574 (11.11.1969), a square section 'O' ring seal and retaining sleeve was added to the lower end of the push rod cover tube to aid oil retention.

A revised breather system required a drive-side crankcase with three holes below the main bearing housing, maintaining a constant oil level in the primary chaincase. To allow engine breathing, the oil seal between the crankcase and the engine sprocket was deleted. A bolt-on right-angle adapter was fitted to the rear of the primary case to take the engine breather pipe along the rear mudguard.

From AD39329 (27.1.1970), the Amal R930/45 Concentric carburettor replaced the R930/23, and now had a cast-in weir and drain plug in the float bowl. The settings remained as before.

Gearbox Also from AD39329, a heavier section circlip was fitted to retain the gearbox mainshaft bearing in the gearbox inner case. From GD53756 (11.6.1970), aluminium bronze selector forks with captive steel rollers replaced the forged steel ones. A precision pressed gear camplate was also fitted. The camplate plunger, spring and plunger housing were replaced by a leaf spring attached to the gearbox inner cover. The selector fork spindle was shortened, fitting into a blind hole in the crankcase, obviating a potential oil leak at this point.

Transmission No change.

Frame A detachable front engine plate was specified from JD26050 (20.8.1969), considerably easing the fitting of the engine to the frame. The bolt-on engine plate required a modified frame for compatibility. The Girling suspension units were also modified, being fitted with castellated spring adjuster sleeves.

Forks From AD39329 (27.1.1970), the wheel spindle cap bolts were replaced by studs and nuts. The mudguard stay fitting pommels were replaced by small welded-on pressings with captive square nuts. The steering stem chrome-plated blind nut was specified for the TR6C, and the steering damper assembly was deleted.

Petrol tank No change.

Technical development

Revised for 1969/70, the new anchor plate, showing altered cam levers, cable abutment and cranked mudguard stay.

For the 1969 season, Ruby Red gave a distinctive finish on the US TR6R. A new cast alloy rear lamp housing, bolt-on passenger grab rail, and straight pull front brake cable, were some of the features.

Oil tank The US models had the rear chain oiling system deleted as it was regarded as an oil leak when the machine was stopped and the residue oil in the feed pipes dripped to the ground.

Brakes A flat strip rear brake torque stay replaced the tubular one.

Wheels The rear hub threaded parts were changed to UNF (previously CEI).

Mudguards In the interests of safety, the front mudguard bottom stay was now fitted with two fixing ears, requiring a new mudguard to match. The rear mudguard was modified to accept the D section engine breather pipe

The Triumph Trophy Bible

Bird's-eye view of the 1969 TR6R. New for 1969 was the blind chromed stem nut which deleted the steering damper.

along the left-hand side. A rear grab rail was now integral with the rear mudguard support stay.

Exhaust No change.

Electrical The smaller Lucas 17M 12v oil-filled ignition coils were specified for all models.

Speedo/tacho The speedometer changed yet again, to SSM/00, and the tachometer to RSM 3003/13.

Handlebars No change.

Seat The threaded bosses for the passenger grab rail were deleted, and a new seat pan pressing allowed a lower seat height.

Toolbox No change.

Extras
Tachometer   £11.7.0
QD rear wheel   £9.10.0

Price £404.5.3

This was the last season the TR6 was fitted with a single down tube frame and separate oil tank. Last models built:

TR6R	KD59715	7.9.1970
TR6C	KD59978	9.9.1970
TR6	KD60018	9.9.1970
TR6P	ND60540	9.10.1970

1971 TR6 Tiger

Engine prefix: TR6R, TR6C, TR6P, TR6RV
Engine numbers: PE003157 to HE029817
Build dates: 3.11.1970 to 8.7.1971

For the 1971 season, the TR6 variants took on a completely new look. Just about every component on the cycle side was new, with the frame containing the engine oil in a large spine tube. Basically, the engine unit remained as before, with modifications relating mainly to the fitting of the engine unit to the frame during assembly.

Technical development

The 1970 UK TR6. These photographs show the passenger grab rail integral with the rear mudguard stay.

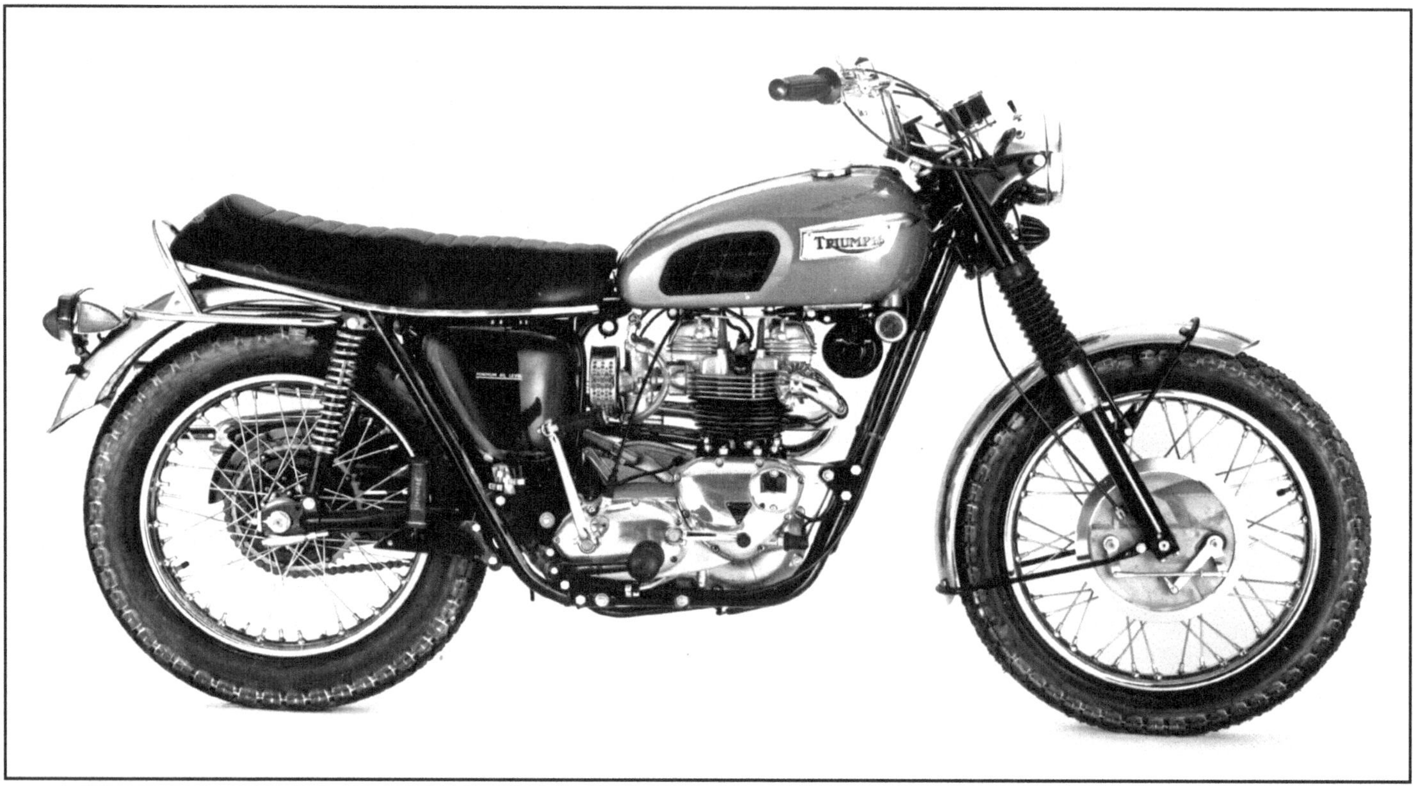

The Triumph Trophy Bible

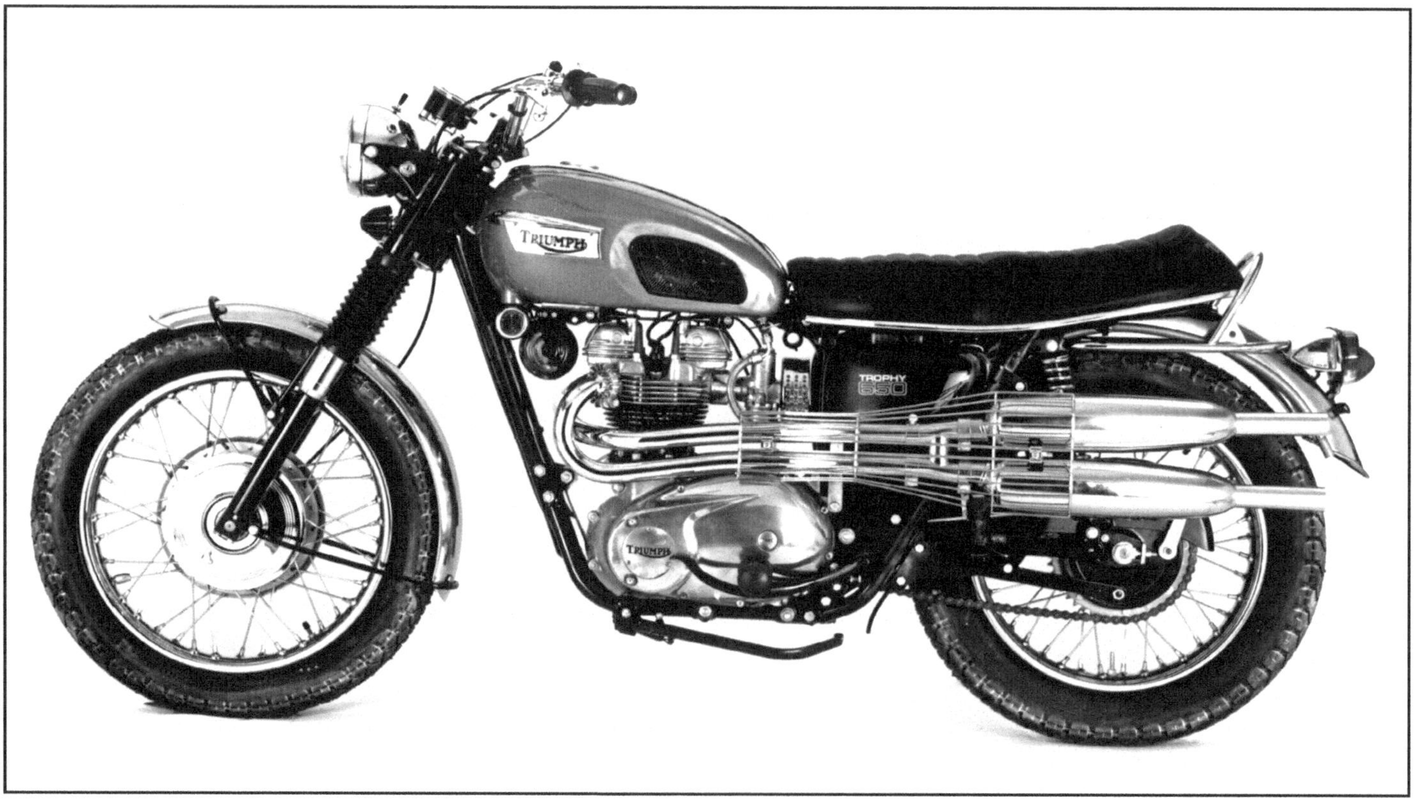

The 1970 Trophy TR6C was very similar to the 1969 model.

Technical development

1970 Trophy TR6R for the US market.

The Triumph Trophy Bible

Engine A new cylinder head, modified to accept the internally ribbed rocker boxes, was required to enable the head to be removed with the engine *in situ*. Two-part cylinder head/rocker box retaining bolts replaced the long one-piece ones.

Modified push rod cover tubes featured a full unbroken rim, with drain hole piercing replacing the castellated pattern. The new rocker boxes were fitted with threaded side plugs adjacent to the rocker adjuster and valve tip. This was to assist with tappet adjustment, whereby a feeler gauge could be inserted between the adjuster and valve tip upon removal of the threaded plug.

A new metric timing side mainbearing was fitted, from GE27029 (19.6.1971), requiring a modified crankshaft and crankcase. The new bearing was a ball journal, 72 x 30 x 19mm, and the crankshaft diameter was amended to 1.1812/1.1808in. The change in the outer diameter of the bearing, from $1^{1}/_{8}$in to 72mm, meant that a new crankcase was required.

Gearbox A five speed gearbox could be specified as an optional extra, from GE027729 (24.6.1971), though the four speed remained as standard fitting.

Transmission A new engine sprocket, without the ground oil seal diameter, was introduced this year. A new spacer and shims of 0.010 and 0.030in were added so that primary chain alignment could be maintained.

Frame The twin down tube, one-piece welded frame was entirely new for the 1971 season. This was a first, since the Triumph Eng. Co. Ltd. had never before used a one-piece frame on any production twin model. The large diameter tubular spine frame served as the oil tank, though with a capacity of only four pints.

The steering head bearings were taper roller, and the swinging arm pivoted on bronze bushes and hardened steel bobbins. Girling suspension units of 12.9in centres with 110lb exposed chrome plated springs were retained.

Forks The entirely new front forks had hard chrome stanchions and bushless alloy bottom members. Alloy wheel spindle caps were retained by four studs and nuts. Small rubber scraper sleeves were fitted at the top of the bottom members to exclude road dirt.

Petrol tank A new rubber-mounted three gallon petrol tank with a single central fixing bolt was fitted. The previous year's tank badges and knee grips were retained. A chrome centre mounting cup, and styling strips fore and aft, finished off the tank.

From the end of the 1971 season, a four gallon petrol tank became available as an option, and subsequently became standard on UK models.

Oil tank Integral within the frame, with a capacity of four pints. The engine feed was taken from the bottom of the frame through a top hat filter.

Brakes The new 8in diameter, twin leading shoe front brake was fitted with a large air scoop. The brake can levers were actuated by a heavy duty bowden cable, the front lever by the inner bowden wire, whilst the rear was operated by the outer casing. A coil spring was fitted between the cam levers on later models when it was discovered that the cable, if slack, could become separated from its seating.

The rear brake featured an aluminium alloy anchor plate, with a short downward-facing cam lever. The original set-up was not very efficient, and the intended 'improvements' were many, including new linings, added fulcrum pads, and a repositioned cam lever and spring. These changes made the rear brake tolerable, but never as good as the previous year's type.

Wheels Both wheels were now of the conical hub type. The material for the hubs was aluminium, with a cast iron liner on which the shoes operated. The rear hub had a 47 tooth sprocket secured by five $^{1}/_{4}$in through-bolts and nuts. Wheel rim size remained as before, *i.e.* WM2 x 19in front and WM3 x 18in rear. Tyres were Dunlop Universal K70 3.25 x 19in front, and 4.00 x 18in rear.

Mudguards Both front and rear mudguards were new for this season. The front was fitted with integral welded-on wire stays mounted in rubber bushes on the fork bottom members. On the UK models, a black plastic front number plate was specified. The TR6C mudguards were chrome plated.

Exhaust system New exhaust pipes to match the new megaphone-shaped silencers were fitted to all models except the TR6C. This model kept the twin upswept pipes and twin round barrel silencers connected by a 'H' piece. The wire 'chip basket' leg guard continued as before.

Air filter Twin rectangular wire mesh/cloth air filters were housed in the aluminium alloy filter box assemblies, and connected directly to the carburettor via a plastic connector.

Electrical A new headlamp with a flat rear shell housed three warning lights: ignition/oil warning; high beam; and a direction indicator light. A two-position rotary switch for selecting pilot and headlamp positions was also fitted.

Lucas direction indicators were controlled by a handlebar console on the right, while a similar switch console on the left operated the horn, headlight dipper and engine cut-out.

The tail lamp continued as before, but was now fitted to a pressed tin housing which also mounted the rear direction indicators. A new Lucas rotary combined ignition and light switch was fitted into the right-hand side panel. A plastic Lucas stop switch was attached to the rear frame tube and operated by the footbrake lever. The ignition coils, rectifier and indicator relay were all grouped together and mounted on a tin pressing under the seat.

Speedo/tacho New Smiths Instruments' SSM 5007/00A 150mph speedometer, and RSM 3003/14 tachometer, were housed in rubber cups attached to the fork top cap nuts by chrome plated ring brackets.

Technical development

1971 Trophy TR6C with chrome plated mudguards.

Handlebars No change to the handlebar bend, but the lever fulcrum brackets were integral with the new Lucas switch consuls

Clutch and brake levers were alloy forgings on the standard TR6, with chrome steel levers fitted to the TR6C. All models had the handlebars mounted in eyebolts fitted into metalastic bushes.

Seat The seat was hinged from the right-hand side, on the opposite side to any previous Triumph. The seat cover was all black, with a ribbed airtex finish on the top, and a black plastic trim band. The seat catch was of the 'ammunition box' pattern on the left side.

Toolbox A tray was provided, integral with the coil tray pressing.

Extras Five speed gearbox.

Price £488.0.0

1972 TR6 Tiger

Engine prefix: TR6R, TR6C, TR6P, TR6RV
Engine and frame numbers: JG033084 to EG057252
Build dates: 20.8.1971 to 17.5.1972

Engine A suffix letter V was added to the engine model code, from CG051405 (24.3.1972), to identify a five speed model. Full-width camshaft pinions were fitted at the same time, which, by eliminating the central threaded boss, avoided possible distortion and gave quieter operation. A new camshaft pinion extractor used the two threaded holes in each pinion. From XG043810 (30.12.1971), the cylinder head was modified to accept 'Push In' exhaust pipe fittings, replacing the threaded steel stubs and 'Push Over' exhaust pipes.

Also from XG043810, new style rocker boxes with flat finned covers retained by four fixing screws gave improved access for tappet adjustment over the previous individual inspection caps. From AG046174 (25.1.1972),

The Triumph Trophy Bible

The 1971 Tiger TR6 was identical to the Trophy TR6C, except for the exhaust system and the painted mudguards.

the cylinder head fixing bolts inside the rocker boxes were changed from having an external hexagon to being cylindrical with an internal hexagon. Previously, the 500 mile service cylinder head retorque required the removal of the rocker boxes. The revised design, however, allowed an Allen key to be inserted through the rocker box, after the upper bolts were removed, so that the fixing bolts could be retorqued.

Gearbox Leaf spring indexing for the gearchange camplate was deleted, and the system reverted back to the spring loaded plunger of pre-1970.

From EG056421 (10.5.1972), the high gear mainbearing on the five speed gearbox changed from a 13 roller to 11, requiring a new high gear to suit since the individual components were not interchangeable.

Transmission From CG 051405, the shock absorber inner and outer plates were secured by three through bolts, peened over to provide locking. This was to overcome persistent loosening of the previous six countersunk screws.

Frame The frame was redesigned to give a lower seat height, and the seat itself was hinged from the left-hand side, reverting to the 1970 condition, as did the seat catch mechanism. The Girling suspension units were shortened from 12.9in to 12.4in.

Modified air filter boxes and side panels, along with a new coil and combined tool tray were required. The petrol tank mounting bolt bracket was reversed so that the open end of the slot faced forwards to accept the new tank fixing bolt (which had a coach bolt type head). All these modifications were from CG051405.

Forks A new bottom yoke and stem assembly was specified, with a 24tpi UNF thread replacing the 16tpi unit, thus enabling finer adjustment of the tapered steering head bearings. A new stem sleeve nut was required for compatibility. Later 1972 season models had the fork bottom members fully polished and the styling rib removed.

Petrol tank No change.

Oil tank The oil reservoir gauze filter was modified. A fixed location plate and a separate sump plate were fitted to provide better sealing.

Brakes No change.

Wheels No change.

Technical development

Mudguards The front mudguard for UK models was lengthened at the front end, and all models had an extra centre stay added to prevent known stay fractures.

Exhaust New exhaust pipes to match the redesigned cylinder head with its 'push in' exhaust ports were specified.

Air filter The fluted alloy air box outer covers were replaced by plain, non-fluted plastic covers, when fitted to the lowered frame.

Electrical To make them more user friendly, the handlebar switches were swapped around. On the left console were the direction indicator switch and the engine cut-out button. The headlamp flasher button, horn push, and dipper switch lever were on the right.

To prevent bracket fractures, the horn was mounted to the frame via two rubber grommets.

Speedo/tacho Smiths' SSM5007/00A speedo continued to be fitted, along with the RSM3003/13A tachometer.

Handlebars No change.

Seat Up to CG051405, a thinner seat cushion was used to reduce the seat height.

Toolbox After CG051405, the tool tray was integrated with the coil tray.

Extras Five speed gearbox.

Price £573.0.0

This was the last year of the TR6C, bringing to an end one of the most popular off road models Triumph had produced. The last TR6C was AG044359, on 5th January 1972.

1973 TR6 and TR7 Tiger

Engine prefix: TR6P, TR6RV, TR7P, TR7RV
Engine and frame numbers: JH15475 to GH35466
Build dates: 18.8.1972 to 15.6.1973

Engine Whilst the TR6 650cc continued as before, a larger engine with a capacity of 724cc (bore and stroke of 75mm x 82mm) was fitted to the TR7. When modified cylinder barrel castings were available from the foundry, the cylinder bore was opened up to 76mm, giving a capacity of 744cc.

Summary
JH15475 to JH15596   TR6RV   650cc
KH17097 to KH17121   TR6P   650cc
KH17122 to XH21715   TR7RV   724cc   75mm

The 1972 Trophy TR6C retained the short chrome plated mudguards.

The Triumph Trophy Bible

For the UK, the 1972 Tiger TR6 featured a longer front mudguard and the four gallon petrol tank.

AH23727 to GH35387	TR7RV	744cc	76mm
GH35388 to GH35466	TR7P	744cc	76mm

Piston/cylinder barrel grading for the 744cc engine followed on from the 650cc system:

	Low	Med	High
Piston (in)	2.9874/71	2.9878/75	2.9882/79
Barrel (mm)	75.973/.980	75.990/.983	76.000/.993

New crankcases with larger barrel mouths were designed to accommodate the larger cylinder bores. Shorter connecting rods, with 6in centres matching the reduced length of the cylinder barrel, were also specified. The crankshaft was modified to give a longer rotor support shaft, to take the triplex engine sprocket, and, at the same time, the crankshaft was given UNF threads.

When the correct specified camshafts were used, the inlet followers were changed to $^3/_4$in (0.750in) radius, while the exhaust stayed at $1^1/_8$in radius. The camshaft pinions carried two sets of stamped timing marks, 'A' and 'B'. When timing the camshafts, the letter B must align with the keyway on the inlet camshaft, and the dash on the intermediate pinion. The letter A mark must align with the keyway on the exhaust camshaft, and the dot mark on the intermediate pinion. The cold running tappet clearances with these camshafts should be 0.008in inlet and 0.006in exhaust. This system was used from XH21257 (15.12.1972), and the camshafts were stamped 71-7016 on the inlet and 71-7017 on the exhaust.

The TR7 was fitted with a new cylinder head with two $^5/_{16}$in central fixings. These, and the four $^3/_8$in studs screwed into the barrel, were special high expansion steel. Sleeve nuts with internal threads and hexagons held the head to the barrel on the four $^3/_8$in studs. Locating dowels between the rocker boxes and cylinder head prevented gasket movement. The rocker box tappet covers were modified, from CH27556 (8.3.1973), to accept six bolt fixing, as were the rocker boxes, preventing oil seepage from the ends of the covers.

A 260 main jet was specified with the larger engines, other settings remained as for the 650 TR6.

Gearbox The five speed layshaft was redesigned with high gear being positively located end-wise by an internal circlip to give constant fourth gear end float. This can be identified by the two turned grooves on the layshaft splined area.

Technical development

To overcome layshaft drive dog and first gear failures, heavy-duty layshaft first, second and third gears were fitted. A much larger, stronger layshaft drive dog (Maltese Cross) was fitted, along with a new layshaft first gear selector fork. None of these new components are interchangeable with the earlier pattern.

A modified camplate was fitted, the early 'fully round' unit being replaced by the 'low inertia' type. The later camplate has the advantage that it can be removed from the gearbox without first having to remove the gearbox sprocket and high gear.

Transmission A triplex primary chain and triple toothed sprockets were fitted on both the TR6 and TR7. The TR7 clutch springs were strengthened to deal with the increased torque. A 20 tooth gearbox sprocket was fitted to the TR7, giving ratios of 4.7, 5.59, 6.58, 8.63, 12.25, and the internal ratios 1.0, 1.19, 1.4, 1.84, 2.6 with the standard five speed gearbox.

Frame The lowered frame continued as 1972. Areas around the centre stand pivot bracket were strengthened, though, to prevent the pivot tube twisting and consequent centre stand failure. The aluminium oil tank sump plate casting incorporated the engine feed oil pipe, which was enlarged to $3/8$in diameter.

Forks For the UK models, rubber gaiters were fitted to protect the fork stanchions from the elements. Fork top covers were fitted with rubber mounted headlamp brackets, the left-hand bracket carried the ignition switch in the same way as the pre-1970 design.

New top and bottom yokes, with wider centres to accommodate the disc-braked wheel, were fitted. The fork stanchions had a parallel top register, fixed to the top yoke by Allen screw clamping. The fork internals remained as before, except that the main spring was shortened to give less preload.

New bottom members with larger diameter spindle bores and wider spaced studs were fitted. The bottom member spindle caps incorporated a threaded lug to mount the mudguard bottom stay. The left-hand member had a triangular casting to mount the hydraulic brake caliper.

The fork top nuts were recessed to allow a motif stating oil type and quantity to be fitted.

Petrol tank Both three and four gallon tanks continued to be available, but the method of attachment, via the centre bolt, was redesigned. The chrome cup and styling strips were deleted. Both tanks lost the centre welds, and the four gallon tank was fitted with metal Triumph badges replacing the silver transfers.

Oil tank As before, except that a dip stick oil indicator was added, integral with the filler cap.

Brakes The front brake was an entirely new disc type unit, hydraulically-operated from a master cylinder mounted on the right handlebar. The 10in diameter cast iron disc was hard chrome plated, and the caliper was a twin piston type by Lockheed Automotives.

The rear brake continued as before.

Wheels A new front wheel was required to accept the disc brake. The hub was polished and lacquered.

The rear wheel remained as before, except for the hub, which was polished and lacquered, and the anchor plate was finished in semi-matt black.

Mudguards Front and rear mudguards were both new for this season. The chrome plated front mudguard featured mounting stays which were very similar to the 1970 tubular ones. The chrome plated rear mudguard was lengthened to give better weather protection.

Exhaust New silencers were specified to comply with increasingly stringent noise level requirements. These were similar to the 1972 megaphone shape, but with reverse taper ends added. This modification entailed the use of new front pipes and silencer mounting brackets.

Air filter The filter covers carried chromed motifs with inset blue and silver model decals.

Electrical The pre-1971 teardrop headlamp shell was reinstated, giving back the traditional Triumph appearance. A three position Lucas 57SA toggle switch was contained within the headlamp shell, as were the previous three warning lights. A Lucas S45 Yale-type on/off ignition switch was positioned in the left-hand headlamp mounting bracket. A Lucas 10CA contact breaker assembly and a Lucas L917 tail lamp with a larger reflective area were fitted. A new polished aluminium housing was required to mount the new lamp. Provision was made for the tail lamp lens to accept side reflectors (only fitted to the US models as standard equipment).

Speedo/tacho No change.

Handlebars A new high-rise handlebar bend (8in) was fitted to the US models, and all handlebars featured a knurled area adjacent to the master cylinder mounting giving a more secure clamping.

Seat No change.

Toolbox No change.

Price
TR6 £499.18
TR7V £597.00

1974 TR7 Tiger

Engine prefix: TR7RV
Engine and prefix numbers: JJ58039 to JJ58064
Build dates: 30.8.1973 to 31.8.1973

Engine The engine breather stub outlet, fitted on the rear face of the primary chaincase, was changed to a black plastic unit, replacing the earlier aluminium component. A new Smiths pressure switch with a nylon insert was also fitted. The cylinder barrel threads were changed to UNF,

The Triumph Trophy Bible

as were the cylinder head fixing bolts.

Gearbox A new high gear with a radial groove to take an 'O' ring seal was specified. To provide a seating for the 'O' ring, the final drive sprocket featured an internal chamber. This modification prevented oil seepage along the high gear splines.

Transmission No change.

Frame No change.

Forks No change.

Petrol tank No change.

Oil tank No change.

Brakes Front - no change. Rear - the brake cam was modified by the introduction of a squared taper fitting for the brake cam lever, replacing the two flats type.

Wheels No change.

Mudguards Heavier gauge brackets mounting the mudguard stays to the fork bottom members were fitted.

Exhaust The longer silencers introduced for 1973 were altered slightly, in that the conical rear end extensions were now a parallel taper, easing production difficulties.

Air filter No change.

Electrical No change.

Speedo/tacho No change.

Handlebars No change.

Seat No change.

Toolbox No change.

Price £616.00.

The last TR7RV built by the Triumph Engineering Co. Ltd. was JJ58064 on 31st August 1973.

1975 TR7 Tiger

Engine prefix: TR7RV
Engine and frame numbers: GK62244 to GK62248
Build date: 26.6.1975

Only five were produced for the 1975 season.

Specification was the same as the 1974 models, but they were now produced wholly by the Co-operative. GK62248 was the last TR7RV to be produced. The gear change pedal was on the right-hand side, and the machine was fitted with a drum rear brake.

Price £805.00.

1976 TR7 Tiger

Engine prefix: TR7RV
Engine and frame numbers: DN70186 to EN71867
Build dates: 13.4.1976 to 26.5.1976

1974 US TR7RV.

Technical development

Engine The compression ratio was reduced from 8.5:1 to 7.9:1, promoting reliability in light of the available fuels.

The crankcase was redesigned to accept the gear change cross shaft, and 'O' ring seals replaced the fibre washers on the oil pressure release valve, the timing plug, and the crankcase filter.

The Amal Concentric carburettor mainjet was increased to 270 from 260.

Gearbox New inner and outer covers were required to accommodate the gear change cross shaft, and to move the gear change pedal over to the left-hand side.

Primary transmission The primary outer cover was redesigned to allow the exit of the gear change cross shaft. The large circular rotor/timing cover was replaced by a small threaded plug and a fixed pointer for ignition timing.

Frame A new frame and swinging arm was specified to accept the hydraulically-operated rear disc brake. The main footrests were altered slightly to make them non-handed.

So as to comply with US regulations, the pillion footrests were pegged to the frame to provide a 45 degree rearwards angle.

Forks No change.

Petrol tank Modified petrol taps with indicator plates were fitted to comply with US regulations.

Oil tank No change.

Brakes The front disc brake continued as per 1973. The rear brake was now an hydraulically-operated disc, though, actuated by a right side foot lever. The brake lever operated a master cylinder fitted under the swinging arm pivot, which, in turn, hydraulically-operated a caliper mounted under the rear wheel spindle.

Wheels Front - no change. The rear wheel was a completely new assembly to accept the bolt on brake disc and rear chain sprocket. Rim size was as before, WM3 x 18in.

Mudguards Front - no change. The rear mudguard was modified to give clearance for the rear brake hydraulic reservoir.

Exhaust system The silencer mounting brackets were now left- and right-handed, with a dog leg offset to give clearance for the rear brake caliper.

Air filter The air filter back plates had pressed square apertures to take plastic air intake tubes to reduce induction noise.

Electrical A new Lucas indicator/dipper switch on the left-hand handlebar required a separate steel clutch lever assembly.

Speedo/tacho The Smiths Instruments SSM4003/00 and RSM3006/00 had the NVT wiggly worm motif on the dial.

Handlebars No change, except for the new clutch lever as mentioned.

Seat Harmonisation of the front and rear seat hinges meant a slight alteration to the seat pan pressing.

Toolbox The tooltray cum ignition coil mounting was modified to accept the rear master cylinder hydraulic reservoir.

Price £805.00.

1977 TR7 Tiger

Engine prefix: TR7RV
Engine and frame numbers: HP74444 to HP84475
Build dates: 14.7.1976 to 13.7.1977

It will be seen from the above that the letters HP, indicating July 1977 season, were also used in July 1976, *i.e.* they were used twice in the one season. For dating purposes, therefore, it could be misleading if only the month codes are used, so the numbers should also be taken into consideration.

Engine From GP84113 (15.6.1977), a 'Klinger' composite eyeleted cylinder head gasket was fitted, replacing the troublesome copper one. This gasket proved oiltight and not prone to failure between the cylinder bores as the copper one had.

The rotor nut tab washer was replaced by a fan disc lockwasher, from HP84416 (9.7.1977). This stopped the nut from slackening and causing crankshaft keyway damage.

The Amal Concentric carburettor was fitted with larger extended float ticklers.

Mudguards A new front mudguard flat plate pressing replaced the tubular front and centre stays. A modified front mudguard with five fixing holes was required to match the new fixing.

Speedo/tacho The NVT wiggly worm motif was deleted from the instrument dials, and the Smiths identification codes for the speedometer and tachometer were now SSM 4003/02 and RSM 3003/23, respectively.

Price £1012.0.

1978 TR7 Tiger

Engine prefix: TR7RV
Engine and frame numbers: PX 02117 to HX 10584
Build dates: 18.11.1977 to 11.07.1978

Engine From XX 03343 (27.12.1977), rocker levers and adjusters changed from CEI thread (26tpi), to UNF (24tpi).

Gearbox A gasket was now specified to fit between

the gearbox inner and outer covers, replacing jointing compound.

Frame Girling 'gas shocks' were fitted, and can be identified by the piston rod being $^3/_8$in diameter.

Forks Due to persistent oil seepage problems, fork oil seals were imported from the USA. These so-called 'self aligning' oil seals and retaining washers will fit retrospectively, and, in view of their success, should be considered when there is an oil seepage problem. The chrome top outer covers, previously only fitted to the US models, became standard on all models.

Petrol tank No change.

Oil tank No change.

Brakes No change.

Wheels Front wheel bearings were now of the twin seal type, thereby giving greater reliability by preventing the ingress of water. The rear wheel rim was modified to accomodate thicker, 9 gauge, spokes and nipples. Both front and rear wheels were fitted with Dunlop TT100 tyres, 4.10 x 19 front and 4.10 x 18 rear.

Mudguards Nylon washers were placed under the screw heads on the front mudguard to prevent damage to the paintwork.

Exhaust No change.

Air filter No change to the actual filter arrangement, but decorative plastic side panels were added, retained by two springs.

Electrical Due to Lucas not being able to continue supplies, a new battery source had to be found, so a Yuasa 12N9-4B-1 battery became standard fitment. An alternative light unit was fitted for some markets, the bulb having a larger flange, and the Lucas blade connections required a new sub-harness.

Speed/tacho Veglia instruments were used in some markets.

Handlebars The twistgrip friction setting device and the full throttle stop adjuster screw were deleted, to comply with US federal regulations.

Seat Restyled seats were used for the 1978 season. For the three gallon tank, a narrow-nosed seat was specified, with a wider-nosed seat for the four gallon tank.

Toolbox No change.

Price £1011.00.

Due to ever stricter emissions regulations in the USA, this was the last year the TR7 was acceptable there.

1979 TR7 Tiger

Engine prefix: TR7RV and TR27
Engine and frame numbers: HA11009 to XA24608
Build dates: 13.07.1978 to 14.12.1979

To combat the very high insurance rates in Germany, a special model was produced for that market only. With a maximum output of no more than 27bhp, favourable insurance rates could be obtained.

Engine New valve guides with circlip grooves for location in the cylinder head were specified. These modified guides required new bottom valve spring cups to suit. The cylinder head valve guide bore was slightly modified, with a chamfer to accept the valve guide circlip.

A breather stub was added to the exhaust rocker box, connecting via a rubber pipe to the oil tank vent pipes. The timing cover to crankcase joint was fitted with a gasket, replacing jointing compound as before. The timing cover fixing screws were changed to the Allen socket-head type, replacing the cross-head screws.

Gearbox A neutral indicator electrical switch was fitted into the gearbox inner cover, and operated by a raised pin on the gear change quadrant. The gear change camplate was modified by having a larger indent in the neutral position, giving a more positive feel when neutral was selected.

Stronger gear change quadrant return springs were fitted from DA20768 (5.4.1979), to obviate gear lever sticking. These springs must only be used in pairs, otherwise gear selection will be upset.

A new clutch lift mechanism, with a lower lift ratio than its predecessor, was fitted to the gearbox outer cover. The new mechanism was identifiable by a letter X stamping on the clutch lift plates, and was made necessary by the handlebar clutch lever having a higher pull ratio. As with the timing cover, Allen screws were fitted.

Transmission Apart from Allen screws being fitted, there were no other changes.

Frame The anti-theft steering lock location was moved from the top of the steering head to the bottom. A tubular housing was welded to the right-hand seat tube to accomodate the seat lock.

Two upright pegs were welded into the right-hand seat tube for helmet attachment.

The footrest rubbers lost the Triumph logo, which had been a feature since 1936, and the new footrest rubbers were left and right-handed.

Forks A new top and bottom crown and stem were specified. The top lug had two threaded bosses for the binnacle attachment. The lower lug now incorporated the anti-theft steering lock.

Petrol tank No change, but the knee grips on the UK tank were deleted.

Oil tank No change.

Technical development

Brakes The front brake master cylinder was redesigned to accept the new Lucas handlebar switches.

Wheels Wheel hubs were polished and lacquered.

Mudguards The breather pipe attachment holes on the rear mudguard were deleted. The mudguard lifting handle was redesigned to form a small luggage carrier. The mudguards were chrome plated for all markets.

Exhaust system No change.

Air filter The revised engine breathing system required modification to the right side air box, which housed a breather tower to recycle the engine fumes into the induction system. New side panels with plastic badges were fitted.

Electrical The negative earth now featured a Lucas electronic pointless ignition system, with a new finned alloy cover replacing the chrome one. A Lucas RM24 10.5 amp alternator, with a new Lucas 3DS rectifier, was specified. The voltage control was by a ZD15 zener diode as before, but was now a negative earth type.

The centre console housed a combined ignition and lighting switch, oil warning, high beam, neutral and indicator warning lights.

New Lucas handlebar switches were also fitted; the left-hand one had an integral fulcrum for the clutch lever, whilst the right-hand one had the twist grip rotor and red engine kill button.

Speedo/tachometer Veglia instruments were fitted as standard, and were mounted in new rubber cups and alloy pods attached to the central binnacle. New cables were required, since the squared cable entry was now metric, whereas the Smiths Instruments' units were imperial.

Handlebars New brake and clutch levers were forged alloy, dog-leg-shaped, and with finger indentations.

Seat Two seat styles were specified, one for the four gallon tank and one for the three gallon. The seat pan catch was modified to provide the locking arrangement for the key-operated barrel lock.

Toolbox No change.

Price £1123.00 to £1385.00.

1980 TR7 Tiger

Engine prefix: TR7RV, TR27
Engine and frame numbers: PB25193 to JB27513
Build dates: 26.11.1979 to 14.08.1980

Engine A major improvement to the lubrication system was the introduction of the four valve oil pump. The modification took the form of secondary ball valves added to both the feed and scavenge sides of the pump body. To house the new pump, a modified timing cover, giving clearance around the pump fixing screws, was required. At GB27300 (18.06.1980), the connecting rod cap nuts were revised, the 14-1202 nuts was deleted, and 60-3761 nuts were fitted, giving a more positive locking.

Gearbox No change.

Transmission The primary chain adjuster was now fitted externally, and took the form of a hexagon-headed bolt. This overcame the problem of oil leaking out of the adjuster hole whilst the chain was being adjusted.

Frame A redesigned swinging arm with increased diameter tubing and pressed steel end plates was featured. Stronger rear chain adjusters with $^5/_{16}$in adjuster bolts went with the new swinging arm.

The pillion footrest mountings moved up 1in, allowing the silencers to go up by the same amount. This gave more clearance when cornering.

A larger tool tray was available since the rear brake fluid reservoir was repositioned inside the right-hand side triangular panel, with access through an aperture in the panel.

Forks The US type fork seals were now retained by circlips, superseding the press fit plain washers. To accomodate the circlips, the bottom members had machined grooves.

Petrol tank The three gallon tank was fitted with a new tank badge, plain Triumph with no background embellishments. The petrol taps were changed to BAP, which, being face sealing, were less prone to leaks than the taper peg type.

Oil tank No change.

Brakes Front - See-through master cylinder reservoir enabled a visual level check to be made. Rear - The caliper was repositioned from under the wheel spindle to above it. This required a new forged aluminium bracket to mount the caliper on, as well as a new torque stay. The rear brake fluid reservoir became the same as that on the front from mid-season.

Wheels A new rear hub assembly was required to accomodate the Veglia speedo drive, which was now fitted on the left-hand side of the hub. A redesigned rear sprocket with a thinner centre area and shorter disc/sprocket bolts was specified. Before this, a Smiths speedo gearbox had been fitted on the right-hand side.

The rear caliper was now fitted with the chrome-plated cover as used on the front brake.

Mudguards The rear mudguard was amended since an indent to clear the rear brake fluid reservoir was no longer needed. The rear lifting handle/luggage rack continued, but was modified to accept rubber-mounted direction indicators.

Exhaust system No change.

Air filters No change.

Electrical No change.

Speedo/tachometer No change.

Handlebars No change.

Seat The seat check wire was deleted, and replaced by a built-in seat stop on the rear seat hinge.

Toolbox Larger capacity.

Price £1545.00

1981 TR7 Tiger

Engine prefix: TR7RV, TR7RVS
Engine and frame numbers: KDA28097 to DDA29398
Build dates: 22.09.1980 to 13.04.1981

One of the most obvious changes for the 1981 season was the introduction of electric starting, available on the Bonneville from 1980.

Engine Due to persistent problems associated with the 'push in' exhaust pipe, the design reverted to the pre-1971 threaded stub type. Redesigned inlet valve guides were specified, and these incorporated seals.
 The TDC location plug was moved to the front of the crankcase, since access to the previously rear-located one wasn't possible when the starter motor was fitted. This meant that a modified flywheel was required.
 The right-hand main bearing was uprated to a twin lipped roller, due to failures of the ball journal bearing. This new roller bearing, NUP306, was fitted from CDA29018 (03.03.1981), and will fit retrospectively to any model from GE27029 (1972).
 The exhaust camshaft pressure fed oiling system was deleted, and the inlet and exhaust tappet blocks harmonised. With deletion of the camshaft oiling system, an opportunity was taken to harmonise the followers, so inlet and exhaust became the $^3/_4$ in radius.

Gearbox No change.

Transmission The clutch plates were all reduced by one gauge in thickness so that seven plain plates and six driven ones could be accommodated. At the same time, the clutch spring strength was reduced, with the aim of giving a lighter clutch action.
 The gear change cross shaft 'O' ring was replaced by an oil seal, fitted in the primary chaincase outer. This entailed a new chaincase, of course, to house the seal.

Frame The rider's footrests were redesigned to incorporate a silent block bush to which the footrest part was mounted, thus providing a resilient mounting to absorb vibration.

Forks No change.

Petrol tank Locking fuel caps were offered as an extra.

Oil tank No change.

Brakes No change.

Wheels No change, but Morris cast alloy wheels could be specified as an optional extra.

Mudguards No change to the actual shape, but the chrome was replaced by stainless steel on both front and rear.

Exhaust system No change.

Air filter No change.

Electrical The ES model was fitted with a revised system to cope with the extra loading the electric start imposed. A 14 amp Yuasa YB14L battery with a three phase 14.5 amp alternator was specified. To cope with the extra output, a three pack zener diode fitted on the AC side of the system was required.
 To aid cold starting, a revised ignition reluctor stator was fitted, giving an improved spark at low engine revolutions. All models benefited from the fitting of a 60/45 watt QH headlamp bulb.

Speedo/tacho No change.

Handlebars No change to the actual handlebar, but Buhm (German) round black plastic mirrors were now a standard fitting.

Seat Due to the taller Yuasa battery, the seat pan required a pressed recess to give the necessary clearance.

Toolbox No change.

Extras The TR7 could now be ordered to any specification, US or UK, with any one of six colour schemes.

Price
TR7RV   £1679.00
TR7RVS   £1770.00

1982 TR7 Tiger

Engine prefix: TR7RV, TR7RVS, TR7T, TR7AV, TR65
Engine and frame numbers: JDA29428 to BDA31917
Build dates: 05.05.1981 to 21.02.1982

Two new models were introduced for the 1982 season. The TR7T was built in very limited numbers and was an attempt to introduce an enduro style model into the range. Generally, it followed the standard Tiger specification, the main differences being wheel size, tyres, mudguards, seat and exhaust system. The other new addition was the TR7AV. This model differed from the standard TR7RV in that the engine was mounted to the frame via bonded rubber blocks, the frame itself was somewhat special, as were certain engine components.

Engine At KDA31298 (02.09.1981), the inlet valve guide seals were replaced by 'O' rings fitted over the inlet valve stems. The inlet guides had the reduced diameter at the

Technical development

The Tiger TR7E/S could be fitted with electric start, as shown on this 1981 model.

top deleted.

On the TR7AV, the balance factor was reduced to 50% to take advantage of the rubber mountings.

Gearbox No change.

Transmission No change.

Frame Marzocchi suspension units gradually replaced the Girling units over the course of the season, due to the fact that Girling had ceased production.

Forks The fork bottom members were now painted semi-matt black. The top headlamp mounting brackets were now located between the upper and lower rubber cups placed over the fork stanchions.

Petrol tank Entirely new, Italian-made petrol tanks were introduced (the UK manufacturer had ceased production). The new tank was fitted with hinged 'flip up' type filler caps, which could be lockable if specified.

Oil tank No change.

Brakes The brake disc diameters were reduced from 10in to 9.8in, and the discs were left unplated. Dunlop 'all weather' sintered brake pads were fitted. Lockheed alloy calipers were specified when the optional twin disc brake assembly was ordered.

The TR7T was fitted with a 7in diameter drum rear brake. This was an SLS design, with rod operation from the footbrake pedal.

Wheels To match the drum rear brake, a new rear hub was required, though the wheel size remained at 18in. A 45 tooth rear sprocket replaced the earlier 47 tooth unit on the TR7RV and TR7RVS.

Tyres The TR7T was shod with Avon Mudplugger 3.00 x 21in front and 4.00 x 18in rear tyres. Avon Roadrunner 4.10 x 19in front and 4.10 x 18in rear tyres were fitted to the TR7RV and RS.

Mudguards The two fixing holes on the rear mudguard for the rear grab rail were replaced by one. The new grabrail deleted the previous luggage rack, but still carried the rear direction indicators, and was now finished in semi-matt black paint.

The TR7T was fitted with self-colour yellow plastic mudguards front and rear. The front one mounted directly to the bottom fork yoke, and had no other stays. The rear was a two part affair shaped to carry the tail lamp and number plate.

Exhaust system No change to the TR7 and RVS. A siamezed low level exhaust running down the left side was fitted to the TR7T. The silencer was formed to exit at high level, and the whole exhaust system was finished in black.

Air filter No change.

Electrical New, rather squarish direction indicators, made by ULO, replaced the earlier Lucas ones. A 60/45 watt sealed beam light unit was specified, fitted to the new black headlamp shell.

A $5\frac{3}{4}$in diameter headlamp with a wire mesh protector was fitted to the TR7T.

Speedo/tacho No change.

The Triumph Trophy Bible

1981 Tiger Trail TR7T.

Handlebars No change.

Seat A three-quarter length seat, with a special ribbed seat top, was fitted to the TR7T.

Toolbox No change.

Extras Twin disc front brake. Lockable petrol filler cap. Morris cast alloy wheels.

1983 TR7 Tiger and TR65

Engine prefix: TR7RV, TR7RVS, TR65T, TR7T
Engine and frame numbers: BEA33009 to AEA34386
Build dates: 15.02.1982 to 07.01.1983

A new addition for the 1983 season was the TR65T. Basically the same as the previous season's TR7T, but with a reduced engine capacity of 650cc.

Engine A crankshaft timing pinion made from EN40 nitrided steel was specified for the ES models, to overcome known tooth failures. From PEA34240 (07.11.1982), one piece spring-assisted oil control piston rings replaced the previous Apex type. This modification was aimed at reducing oil consumption.

Gearbox A redesigned mainshaft with larger ($^5/_8$in) diameter threaded ends was introduced at DEA33143 (02.04.1983). This modification required new lockwashers and retaining nuts.

Frame Paioli rear suspension units were fitted to TR7RV and RVS models, whilst Marzocchi units were fitted to the TR65T and TR7T.

These were the only changes made before the factory closed, and no more Tiger models would be produced at Meriden, the birthplace of the Trophy. The last Tiger to be produced was AEA34386, on 7th January 1983.

Chapter 4

1961-1974 unit construction 490cc

1961 TR5AC, 1962 T100SC, 1966 T100C, 1972 TR5T year on year model description

The TR5AC was the first competition model to use unit construction in twin cylinder form.

Based on the model Twenty One, which was introduced in 350cc form at the 1957 Show, the TR5AC was fitted with the enlarged 490cc engine.

The completely new TR5AC weighed some 40lb less than the 1957 pre-unit Trophy it replaced, a very desirable feature when used in competition events.

This 490cc TR5AC model was an immediate success, winning gold medals in European International Six Day Trial events, and found favour in the US in enduro and cross country races.

Although the TR5AC had a very short life, only offered for the 1961 season, it set the pattern for the next decade. For the 1962 season, the 490cc competition model was designated T100SC, and later the T100C.

1961 TR5AR, TR5AC technical data

Engine
Bore	69mm (2.716)
Stroke	65.5mm (2.578)
Capacity	490cc (30cu.in)
bhp	34 @ 7000rpm
Compression ratio	9.0:1

Cylinder head
Material	Aluminium alloy
Valve seat angle	45 degrees
Valve seat width	
Inlet	0.050/0.060in
Exhaust	0.060/0.080in
Valve guide bore	0.4980/0.4985in
Valve stem diameter	
Inlet	0.3095/0.3100in
Exhaust	0.3090/0.3095in
Valve head diameter	
Inlet	$1^7/_{16}$in
Exhaust	$1^5/_{16}$in
Valve guides	
Material	Chilled cast iron
Bore diameter	0.312/0.313in
Outside diameter	0.5005/0.5010in
Length, in. and ex.	1.750in
Valve springs	
Free length outer	$1^1/_2 \pm {^1/_{16}}$in
Free length inner	$1^{19}/_{32} \pm {^1/_{16}}$in
Fitted load	63lb

Camshafts
Journal diameter	
left hand	0.8100/0.8105in
right hand	1.4355/1.4360in
End float	0.013/0.020in
Lobe height	
inlet 0.314in (TR5AC), 0.314in (TR5AR)	
exhaust 0.296in (TR5AC), 0.314in (TR5AR)	
Bush diameter	
left hand	0.8125/0.8135in
right hand	1.4370/1.4375in
Bush length	
left hand, in.	1.0940/1.1014in
left hand, ex.	0.9220/0.9420in

Cylinder barrel
Material	Cast iron
Bore diameter	2.7160/2.7165in
Max. tolerable wear	0.007in
Tappet guide bore	0.9985/0.9990in

Tappet Block
Outer diameter	0.9995/1.000in

The Triumph Trophy Bible

Tappet stem bore	0.3120/0.3125in

Pistons
Clearance in cylinder at maximum dia. (90 degrees to gudgeon pin)	0.0030/0.0045in
Gudgeon pin bore dia.	0.6882/0.6886in
Fitted load	63lb

Cam followers
Foot radius	.750 (3/4in)
Stem diameter	0.3110/0.3115in
Overall length (nominal)	2.775in

Running valve clearances
Inlet	0.002in
Exhaust	0.004in

Valve timing (checked with 0.020 in tappet clearance)

		TR5AR	TR5AC
IVO	BTDC	34 degrees	34 degrees
IVC	ABDC	55 degrees	55 degrees
EVO	BBDC	55 degrees	48 degrees
EVC	ATDC	34 degrees	27 degrees

Push rods
Material	Solid aluminium alloy with end caps at top only
Overall length	4.820/4.845in

Rockers
Bore diameter	0.4375/0.4380in
Spindle diameter	0.4355/0.4360in

Gudgeon pin
Diameter	0.6880/0.6882in
Length	2.151/2.5156in

Piston rings
Ring width	
Compression	0.0615/0.0625in
Scraper	0.1240/0.1250in
Ring gap in cylinder	
Compression	0.0100/0.0140in
Scraper	0.0100/0.0140in
Clearance in piston groove	
Compression	0.0010/0.0030in
Scraper	0.0010/0.0025in

Connecting rods
Small end diameter	0.6905/0.6910in
Big end diameter	1.4385/1.4390in
Side clearance fitted	0.0130/0.0170in
Length between centres	5.3110/5.3130in
Big end bearing	Vandervell

Crankshaft
Crankpin diameter	1.4375/1.4380in
End float fitted	nil with rotor nut tight
Balance factor	52%
Left hand main bearing journal	1.1805/1.1808
Right hand main bearing journal	1.4375/1.4380
Left hand main bearing journal	72 x 30 x 19mm ball
Right hand main bearing bush ID	1.4390/1.4385in

Oil pump
Bore diameter	
Feed	0.3748/0.3753in
Scavenge	0.4372/0.4377in
Plunger diameter	
Feed	0.3744/0.3747in
Scavenge	0.4369/0.4372in
Spring length	1/2in
Ball diameter	7/32in
Drive block width	0.4970/0.4980in

Oil pressure release valve
Pressure release	60lb/sq.in
Spring length	1 3/8in
Idling oil pressure	25lb/sq.in

Carburettor
Type	Amal Monobloc 376/273
Main jet	190
Needle jet	.106
Needle	C
Needle position	3
Throttle valve	3 1/2
Pilot jet	25
Bore	1in

Ignition
Timing	38 degrees/.333in (fully advance)
Points gap	0.014/0.016in
Distributor	Lucas 18 D2 clockwise
Advance range	10 degrees
Spark plug	Champion N5
Plug gap	0.020in
Plug reach	3/4in

Clutch
Friction plates	6
Plain plates	6
Pressure spring	4
Pressure spring free length	1.400/1.500in
Bearing rollers	20
diameter	0.2495/0.2500in
length	0.2310/0.02360in
Hub bearing diameter	1.3733/1.3743in
Sprocket bore diameter	1.0745/1.0755in
Clutch rod diameter	3/16in
Clutch rod length	9.562/9.567in
Clutch plate segment thickness	3/32in
Engine sprocket	26
Clutch sprocket	58
Gearbox sprocket AR 19 tooth	AC 17 tooth

1961-1974 unit construction 490cc

Clutch operating mechanism
  Spring length $^{13}/_{32}$in
  Ball diameter $^{3}/_{8}$in

Kickstart
  Spindle diameter   1.0600/1.0605in
  Spindle bore diameter   1.0620/1.0625in
  Ratchet spring free length $^{1}/_{2}$in

Gearchange mechanism
  Quadrant plunger
    diameter   0.3402/0.3412in
  Plunger bore diameter   0.3427/0.3437in
  Plunger spring number
    of coils   16
  Plunger spring free length $1^{1}/_{16}$in

Footchange spindle
  Right hand diameter   0.6210/0.6215in
  Bush diameter   0.6230/0.6240in

Quadrant springs
  Free length $1^{7}/_{8}$in
  Number of coils   18

Camplate plunger
  Plunger diameter   0.4360/0.4365in
  Housing bore   0.4375/0.4380in
  Spring length $2^{1}/_{2}$in
  Number of coils   22

Mainshaft
  Bearing left hand   30 x 62 x 16mm ball journal
  Bearing right hand   17 x 47 x 14mm ball journal
  Mainshaft diameter left hand   0.7495/0.7500in
  Bush diameter ID   0.7520/0.7530in
  Bush diameter OD   0.9100/0.9120in
  Bush length $2^{19}/_{32}$in

Layshaft
  Bearing diameter left
    hand (needle) $^{11}/_{16}$ x $^{7}/_{8}$ x $^{3}/_{4}$in
  Layshaft diameter left hand   0.6845/0.6850in
  Layshaft diameter right hand   0.6870/0.6875in
  Layshaft O/A length $5^{3}/_{8}$in
  Bush bore right hand   0.6890/0.6900in
  Bush O.D right hand   0.8125/0.8130in

Number of teeth on pinions
Wide ratio 1st condition H18635 to H23103 TR5AR

Mainshaft		Layshaft	Internal ratio
27	4th	17	1.0
28	3rd	23	1.3
23	2nd	28	1.94
18	1st	33	2.88

Standard ratio 1st condition H18635 to H23103 TR5AR

Mainshaft		Layshaft	Internal ratio
26	4th	18	1.0
28	3rd	23	1.19
23	2nd	28	1.76
19	1st	32	2.43

Overall ratios

Standard TR5AR		Wide TR5AC
5.04	4th	5.64
6.00	3rd	7.33
8.88	2nd	10.94
12.26	1st	16.24

Chains
  Primary $^{3}/_{8}$ x $^{1}/_{4}$in x 78 link duplex endless
  Secondary $^{5}/_{8}$ x $^{3}/_{8}$in x 102 link

Frame
  Steering head bearings
    Top   24 x $^{3}/_{16}$in diameter ball
    Bottom   24 x $^{3}/_{16}$in diameter ball
  Swinging arm pivot
    Bush bore   0.8745/0.8750in
    Spindle diameter   0.8735/0.8740in
    Maximum side play   0.0150in
    Frame head angle   67 degrees

Rear suspension
  Unit type   Girling SB4 4164
  Length between centres   12.9in
  Spring colour   Green/green - 100lb
  Spring free length   8.4in

Front fork
  Stanchion diameter   1.3025/1.3030in
  Stanchion length   22in
  Top bush inner diameter   1.3065/1.3075in
  Top bush outer diameter   1.4980/1.4990in
  Top bush OA length   0.995/1.005in
  Bottom bush inner diameter   1.2485/1.2495in
  Bottom bush outer diameter   1.4935/1.4915in
  Bottom bush OA length   0.8700/0.8750in
  Fork leg bore   1.4980/1.5000in
  Spring free length $17^{3}/_{4}$in yellow
  Spring wire diameter   0.160in

Wheels
  Rim size front   WM2 x 19in
  Rim size rear   WM3 x 18in

Tyres
  Front   TR5AC 3.25 x 19 Trials Universal
     TR5AR 3.25 x 19 Ribbed
  Rear   TR5AR 3.50 x 18 Universal Goldseal
     TR5AC 4.00 x 18 Trials Universal

Wheel bearings
  Front   20 x 47 x 14mm ball journal

Rear	20 x 47 x 14mm ball journal
Rear QD	$^3/_4$ x $1^{27}/_{32}$ x $^9/_{16}$in taper roller
Rear QD drum	7/8 x 2 x 9/16in ball journal

Spokes

Front	40 x 6in UH straight 10 SWG
Rear	20 x 10 SWG $7^9/_{16}$in UH left hand
	20 x 10 SWG $7^9/_8$in UH right hand

Wheel offset

Front WM2	
Dimension from drum edge to edge of rim	$^3/_{16}$in
Rear WM3	
Dimension from outer edge of hub to edge of rim	$1^3/_4$in
Rear QD WM3	
Dimension from outer edge of hub to edge of rim	$^7/_8$in
Speedometer gearbox	Smiths

Electrical TR5AC

Alternator	Lucas RM19ET
Voltage	6 volt
Earth	positive
Horn	Clearhooter A585 6 volt
Bulb main	24/24W
Bulb speedo	3W
Bulb stop/tail	6/18W
Ignition coil	2 ET
Distributor	Lucas 18D2 5 degree range

Dimensions

Wheelbase	$53^1/_2$in
O/A length	$83^1/_4$in
O/A width	27in
Seat height	31in
Weight	323lb
Ground clearance	$7^1/_2$in

Capacities

Petrol tank	$2^1/_4$ gallon TR5AC
	3 gallon TR5AR
Oil tank	6 pint
Gearbox	$^2/_3$ pint (375cc)
Primary case	$^1/_2$ pint (300cc)
Telescopic forks	$^1/_4$ pint (150cc)

Lubrication

Engine	
Summer	20-50 SAE
Winter	20-50 SAE
Gearbox	EP 90
Primary case	20 SAE
Telescopic forks	20 SAE

Torque settings

Flywheel bolts	33lbft
Connecting rod nuts	27lbft
Cylinder head bolts	18lbft
Clutch centre nut	50lbft
Mainshaft nut	40lbft
Rotor fixing nut	30lbft
Stator fixing nut	20lbft
Gearbox sprocket nut	80lbft
Camshaft pinion nuts	50lbft
Crankshaft pinion nut	50lbft
Fork stanchion top nuts	80lbft

Left hand threads

Camshaft pinion nuts
Tacho drive securing bolt after H57082

1961 Model TR5AC Trophy

Engine/frame numbers: H18635 to H23103
Build dates: 1.9.1960 to 20.4.1961

Engine The 490cc unit construction engine/gearbox was fitted with a one-piece forged steel crankshaft, to which was fitted a cast iron flywheel held by three fixing bolts. The right hand mainbearing was a steel backed, copper, lead lined, plain bearing bush, through which oil was pressure fed into the crankshaft.

Alloy con rods were fitted with bushed small ends and Vandervell shell big end bearings.

Camshafts were the sports type (3134 inlet/3325 exhaust), operating $^3/_4$in radius followers. The camshafts ran directly in the crankcase, on the right-hand side, with thin wall steel-backed bushes fitted in the left-hand crankcase. The inlet camshaft operated the timed breather valve on the left, and the distributor through a 90 degree skew gear midway along the shaft. The familiar oil pump and drive were retained, drive being through the inlet pinion fixing nut eccentric pin and drive block.

The cylinder barrel was high grade cast iron, fitted with 9.0:1 compression ratio pistons. The aluminium alloy cylinder head was fitted with cast iron valve guides and a bolt on alloy inlet manifold.

The alternator was carried in the primary chaincase, with the rotor pegged to the engine sprocket to give more accurate timing for the energy transfer ignition system.

Gearbox The Triumph-manufactured four speed gearbox was fitted with either standard or wide ratio gears, with the main housing integrated within the engine crankcase. The positive stop mechanism was housed in the gearbox outer cover, as was the clutch lift mechanism. The latter took the form of a quick thread scroll operating in a cast alloy housing.

Primary transmission The multi-plate clutch, fitted with the Langite friction material, continued as for other models. The clutch sprocket was made of cast iron, with a twin set of teeth to accommodate the duplex primary chain. The endless duplex chain was adjusted by a neoprene-backed spring blade tensioner, via a threaded rod.

1961-1974 unit construction 490cc

The 1961 TR5A/C was the first of the twin cylinder unit construction competition models.

The Triumph Trophy Bible

This 1961 TR5A/R is the road-going version of the TR5A/C.

The first unit 500cc competition model, subsequently modified to produce the 1961 TR5A/C.

1961-1974 unit construction 490cc

1961 TR5A/C frame stiffener strut and tank mounting.

Frame An entirely new lightweight cradle frame was fitted, originally introduced for the model Twenty-One. The swinging arm was controlled by hydraulically damped Girling suspension units, with three position spring setting adjusted by a cam at the bottom end of the spring seating.

The easy lift centre stand was fitted to the TR5AR, along with a side stand on the lower left frame tube. The TR5AC was not fitted with a centre stand ex-works, but the fittings were featured on the frame, so one could be added at the owner's discretion.

Forks The telescopic forks featured two-way hydraulic damping, with the top fork covers having ears for the headlamp mounting. The fork stanchions were protected by gaiters fitted above the bottom members. The Triumph steering damper, which operated friction discs at the lower end, was still featured.

Petrol tank The TR5AR petrol tank was used as a stressed member, bolted between the steering head lug and the seat lugs. On the TR5AC, a bolted-in tubular strut replaced the internal tank stiffener, and the tank sat on rubber blocks held in place by a rubber strap stretched over the tank front to rear.

Oil tank The separate five pint oil tank was bolted directly to the rear subframe, with the filler cap hidden under the twin seat.

Rocker oiling was by a branched 'twig', incorporated in the return oil pipe.

Brakes Both brakes were of 7in diameter and of the floating shoe type. The front hub was a full width cast iron unit, with a chrome styling cover on the left hand side. The rear brake drum was integral with the 43 tooth rear sprocket.

Wheels The front hub was laced into a WM2 x 19 rim taking straight spokes, whilst the rear had a WM3 x 18 rim.

Tyres Dunlop 3.25 x 19in and 4.00 x 18 Trials Universals were fitted to the TR5AC, and Dunlop Ribbed 3.25 x 19 and 3.50 Universals shod the TR5AR.

Mudguards Both models were fitted with mild steel sports type mudguards. The front had a tubular stay at the front, followed by a flat strip stay between the fork legs. At the lower end, the mudguard was retained by a front stand as usual.

The rear mudguard was the usual Triumph sports pattern, supported by a curved rear loop and carrying the rear number plate.

Exhaust system The TR5AC featured a siamezed low level pipe terminating into a single barrel-type silencer on the right side. The TR5AR featured twin low level pipes terminating into barrel shaped silencers with offset entries.

Air filter The round body air filter with chromed perforated band was attached directly to the carburettor.

The Triumph Trophy Bible

A gold medal winning unit construction 490cc, based on the TR5A/C. This machine was ridden by Roy Peplow in the 1961 ISDT.

Electrical A Lucas RM 13/15 AC energy transfer alternator was fitted, supplying power for ignition and direct lighting on the TR5AC. The TR5AR was fitted with a similar system, but in this case four of the stator coils charged a battery through a full wave rectifier. The ignition remained direct from the alternator. The battery was a Lucas 6 volt MLZ9E.

Both models were fitted with a Lucas 18D2 distributor with an advance range of 5 degrees. A $5^{3}/_{4}$in headlamp with black painted shell was fitted to the TR5AC, this shell contained a push dip switch, and a 24/24W pre-focus light unit operated by a rotary switch.

The TR5AR was fitted with the normal Lucas SS700P 7in chrome headlamp, with a 30/24 pre-focus light unit. The headlamp shell containing the ammeter only.

The horn was a Lucas 8HAC for the TR5AC, and a normal 8H direct for the TR5AR. The stop switch for both models was a Lucas 65A 34279, D-shaped.

The Triumph patent rear number plate carried a Lucas 564 combined stop/tail lamp, with a 6 volt/18 watt bulb for both models.

The ignition coil for the energy transfer system was a Lucas 2ET single unit.

1961-1974 unit construction 490cc

This photo shows a works 490cc Scrambles model, of 1961 vintage.

On the TR5AR, the combined horn/dip switch was the normal Triumph chrome unit mounted on the clutch lever bracket.

Speedometer The TR5AC took a Smiths SC5301/09 speedometer, the TR5AR a SC5301/03 unit. Both were mounted on the fork top lug and featured plain dials.

Handlebars Semi hi-rise $7/8$in diameter handlebars rigidly mounted onto the top fork lug. Amal twistgrip and control levers with ball ends were fitted to both models.

Built-in cable adjusters were fitted on both clutch and brake levers.

Seat A twinseat with a black top and side cover, white piping and black band, was hinged on the left-hand side. A removable chrome knurled knob locked the seat down, whilst a Bowden cable strap restrained the upward movement. Hinges were the forged fabricated type.

Extras
   QD rear wheel   £4.2.10

Pillion footrests	£1.2.9
Twinseat safety straps	£0.11.6

1962 Model Trophy T100S/C

Engine/frame numbers: H26772 to H28552
Build dates: 29.12.1961 to 12.5.1962

The 1961 TR5AC and TR5AR were discontinued for the 1962 season. The TR5AC became the T100SC, and the TR5AR emerged as the T100SS. For the purpose of this book only the T100C Trophy will now be considered. Anyone seeking more details on the T100 unit should consider John Nelson's book, *Triumph Tiger 100/Daytona*.

Engine The four outer cylinder head fixing bolts had the hexagon head lengthened to give better spanner access. The rest of the engine specifications remained as 1961.

Gearbox A 23 teeth mainshaft high gear, with much coarser, stronger teeth, was fitted. A 14 teeth layshaft high gear was fitted to match. These modifications were aimed at preventing tooth breakage, and gave a wider ratio spread (fitted from H26772). This modification gave new ratios of:

Internal		Overall
1.0	4th	5.64
1.35	3rd	7.61
2.00	2nd	11.28
3.01	1st	16.97

Transmission As 1961.

Frame As 1961.

Forks As 1961.

Petrol tank The normal 'basket weave' badge was fitted, replacing the 'Cub' type.

Oil tank As 1961.

Brakes As 1961.

Wheels As 1961.

Tyres As 1961.

Mudguards As 1961.

Exhaust system As 1961.

Air filter As 1961.

Electrical As 1961.

Speedo Smiths SC3304/11.

Handlebars As 1961.

Seat The seat cover now had a grey top, black sides, and a grey trim lower band.

1963 Model T100S/C

Engine/frame numbers: H30214 to H30284
Build dates: 23.10.1962 to 25.10.1962

As can be seen from the model numbers and build dates, very few T100S/C models were built this season. In fact, only 70, possibly the lowest build quantity in the history of the Trophy to date. With so few T100S/Cs being produced, changes were few, so only those applicable are listed.

Engine The most obvious change was the new timing cover which now carried the auto advance unit and the CB points under a chrome circular cover. The auto advance unit was driven by the exhaust camshaft which now carried an internal taper. A 0.024in thick cylinder head gasket replaced the 0.040in one to combat the copper shortage at the time.

The rocker box caps now had serrated edges to match the retaining clips. The flywheel retaining bolt washers were deleted, and Loctite was used to retain the bolts.

Petrol tank The tank now had recesses on the underside to accommodate the relocated coils. New mountings for the petrol tank took the form of four bolts (one at each corner), and rubber buffers. These were attached to flat strips held to the main frame tube by U bolts and nuts.

Oil tank A new oil tank, retaining the five pint capacity, was rubber mounted and fitted with a Ceandes cam action filler cap.

Brakes The integral drum/sprocket now carried 46 teeth, replacing the 43 tooth unit.

Exhaust system A siamezed high level exhaust pipe running over the primary chaincase terminated in a small round barrel silencer. A leg shield was attached to the exhaust pipe.

Air filter The perforated chrome filter band now had an unpierced upper part to prevent water ingress.

Gearbox The gearchange camplate was 'bridged', joining the outer track to the inner, to avoid 'spreading', and the subsequent jumping out of gear. An 18 tooth sprocket replaced the earlier 17 tooth unit, to compensate for the larger 46 tooth rear wheel sprocket. This gave overall ratios of 5.7, 7.69, 11.4, and 17.15.

Transmission A new three vane shock absorber was featured, improving shock absorption. This required new spring pins, springs and cups, as well as a new pressure plate.

Frame A new front frame was featured, but the only real difference was that small triangular brackets were welded to the top tube to carry the twin ignition coils. The rear

1961-1974 unit construction 490cc

The 1963 T100S/C complete with side panels, upswept exhaust system, and wide ratio gearbox.

frame was redesigned to accept the rubber mounted oil tank and new tool tray.

Forks To harmonise with other models in the range, the fork springs were changed to $17^{11}/_{16}$ overall length, 0.160in wire diameter. Black/green colour code.

Electrical The newly introduced timing cover carried the Lucas 4CA contact breaker assembly. The 5 degree auto-advance cam was driven from the end of the exhaust camshaft, replacing the inlet camshaft driven distributor.

The 4CA system required the use of twin coils (Lucas 3ET), and these were mounted below the fuel tank on the main frame tube.

A Lucas 31383 pull-type stop switch replaced the 6SA 'D'-type.

Speedo As 1962.

Handlebars The previous handlebars were retained, but now carried a Lucas S5 cut-out button, shorting out both coil feeds, as an engine kill switch.

Extras
QD rear wheel	£4.9.5
Pillion footrests	£1.4.0
Twinseat safety strap	£0.12.6

1964 Model T100S/C

Engine/frame numbers: H32793 to H35489
Build dates: 9.10.1963 to 23.6.1964

Engine The only change to the engine specification was to the lower push rod cover sealing, whereby metal cups aided the retention of the white, square-section 'O' rings.

Gearbox A completely new gear cluster was introduced, with the layshaft being supported fully on needle roller bearings instead of plain bushes. The new gear cluster had a redesigned tooth giving greater root strength, and, due to the number of teeth on each gear, gave slightly different internal ratios:

MS		LS	internal ratio	overall ratio
23	4th	14	1.0	5.82
24	3rd	20	1.37	7.97
20	2nd	24	1.97	11.46
15	1st	29	3.18	18.5

Layshaft bearing right-hand (needle) $5/_8$ x $^{13}/_{16}$ x $^3/_4$in.

The clutch lift mechanism became common to the other Triumph models, using the pressed steel ramps and three ball method. A huge benefit with the new lift mechanism, was the ability to change the clutch cable without having first to remove the gearbox outer cover. To allow this, the new system was fitted with a 'spoke' and nipple arrangement, in a tower on the gearbox outer cover.

Frame Slight modifications to the rear subframe, in the form of small triangular-shaped brackets welded to the lower end of the seat tubes, replaced the welded tubes taking the pillion footrests. A crankcase undershield was

The Triumph Trophy Bible

This works scrambler was built for John Giles in 1964.

1961-1974 unit construction 490cc

1964 T100SC with obligatory passenger seat strap.

added to the specification.

Forks Redesigned forks with external springs and large chrome seal holders were featured. The external springs were covered by rubber gaiters, retained by metal straps. A rubber bush was fitted inside the steering stem to prevent the steering damper knob unwinding.

Petrol tank As 1963.

Oil tank As 1963.

Electrical As 1963.

Speedometer The chronometric speedo was replaced by the new Smiths 'anti vibration' magnetic type (SSM 5001/00, grey centre spot, black dial with white figures and orange pointer). This new speedo required a redesigned mounting bracket and a new drive cable, as the cable retaining nut differed from the chronometric type. The tacho (RSM3001/02) was of the same style as the speedo.

Handlebars As 1962.

Seat As 1963.

Brakes As 1963

Wheels As 1963.

Tyres T100C models for the East Coast (Tri-Cor), were fitted with Dunlop Trials Universal 3.50 x 19in front and 4.00 x 18in rear, or Dunlop Sports 4.00 x 18in rear. The West Coast (Jomo) machines had Dunlop K70 Gold Seal Universals, 3.25 x 19in front and 4.00 x 18in rear.

Mudguards The mudguards were now made from aluminium alloy, polished to a high finish. The front centre stay flat strip was replaced by a tubular stay, and fixed to the bottom members by individual pear-shaped brackets.

Exhaust system As 1963.

Air filter As 1963.

Extras

QD rear wheel	£4.9.5
Pillion footrests	£1.4.0
Twinseat safety strap	£0.15.4
Tachometer	£7.16.0

1965 Model T100S/C

Engine/frame numbers: H36434 to H40098
Build dates: 23.9.1964 to 5.6.1965

Engine The oil pressure indicator button and shaft was replaced by a blind domed cap nut, and, at the same time, a single spring replaced the two previously fitted.
The crankshaft flywheel now featured a milled slot

The Triumph Trophy Bible

The T50WD *circa* 1965. The machine featured a mix of Trophy and Speed Twin components. Only seventeen were built as the contract was awarded to BSA.

in its periphery to locate the crankshaft at top centre. A threaded hole in the rear of the crankcase was provided to take a service tool which then locked into the flywheel, ensuring that top centre was positively located.

Gearbox As 1964.

Primary transmission As 1964.

Frame As 1964.

Forks A redesigned front fork was introduced, to overcome the limited travel of the 1964 type. New, one inch shorter, bottom sliders, 22in stanchions, and longer $9^3/_4$in springs with a wire diameter of 0.160in (yellow/blue code), were also specified. The gaiters and gaiter clips remained as before. The new bottom members were made by extrusion, and required new front wheel spindle clamps. The front brake cable abutment on the right-hand bottom member was deleted.

Petrol tank As 1963.

Oil tank As 1964.

Brakes The front brake anchor plate shoe fulcrum pin bore diameter was enlarged, to provide centering adjustment to compensate for loading shoe wear. The

The 1965 T100SC featured alloy mudguards, direct battery-less ignition and lighting. The ugly tail lamp extension was required to meet US regulations.

1961-1974 unit construction 490cc

fulcrum pin was lengthened to take the front brake cable abutment.

The rear anchor plate bore was increased in diameter, to allow for brake shoe centralisation by slackening the backplate retaining nut and applying the brake.

Wheels The front wheel spindle was redesigned to suit the new front fork end caps. The quickly detachable rear wheel hub taper roller bearings were replaced by ball journal bearings, $3/4 \times 1^{7}/_{8} \times {}^{9}/_{16}$in.

Tyres A Dunlop Sports 3.0 x 19in tyre was added to the options list for the East Coast machines when the Dunlop Sports 4.00 x 18in rear was fitted.

Mudguards As 1964.

Exhaust system As 1964.

Air filter As 1963.

Electrical As 1963.

Speedo As 1964.

Handlebars As 1962.

Seat As 1963.

1966 Model T100 S/C

Engine/frame numbers: H40528 to H48215
Build dates: 8.7.1965 to 17.6.1966

Engine To obviate the rear chain jamming around the gearbox sprocket in the event of chain failure, a protector guide was introduced, shrouding the gearbox sprocket.

Gearbox As 1964.

Transmission As 1964, except that the clutch pressure plate adjuster was increased in diameter to $3/_{8}$in, entailing a new pressure plate, clutch rod adjuster screw and nut.

Frame A new front and rear frame was introduced for the 1966 season. The front frame now had the previously bolted-in top tube welded in as a permanent fixture. The rear frame was modified with different oil tank and battery mounting brackets.

Forks The forks continued as 1965, but the East Coast models specified additional internal piston and rod dampers, and heavy duty springs ($9^{3}/_{4}$in overall length, coded yellow/green, with 0.212in wire diameters).

Petrol tank A new petrol tank was introduced. It featured new style winged bird tank badges and no tank-top luggage grid.

Oil tank The oil tank was now fully rubber mounted, and had a rear chain lubricator, adjustable by a taper needle screw, fitted within the filler cap neck. The rocker feed take-off was relocated to the top of the oil tank.

Brakes As 1965.

Wheels As 1965, except that the 46 tooth integral drum and sprocket was deleted in favour of a bolt-on 46 tooth sprocket.

Tyres As 1965.

Mudguards As 1964.

Exhaust system As 1963.

The 1966 T100C featured the new bird wing tank badge and cast alloy tail lamp housing. Polished alloy mudguards were specified on west coast Jomo models.

The Triumph Trophy Bible

Timing side view of the 1966 T100C.

Air filter As 1963.

Electrical A new Lucas tail lamp, type L679, was fitted to a new aluminium alloy tail lamp housing.

Speedo/tacho Some T100C models sold in the US were fitted with VDO enduro-type speedos by the distributors. A tachometer was now offered as an optional extra.
  Speedo: Smiths SM5001/00A, tacho: Smiths RSM 3003/01A.

Handlebars The only change was the fitting of white fluted handlebar grips.

Seat As 1963.

Toolbox As 1964.

1967 Model T100C Sports Tiger

Engine/frame numbers: H49834 to H57082
Build dates: 29.8.1966 to 30.6.1967

Engine The Triumph-manufactured pistons were replaced by Hepworth and Grandage parts. The compression ratio remained at 9.0:1. The oil pump scavenge plunger diameter was increased from 0.437in to 0.487in, to ensure crankcase oil level was maintained.

Gearbox The gearbox mainshaft now featured UNF threads, and the clutch end was lengthened to take a self locking Philidas nut and plain washer.

Transmission As 1966.

Frame An entirely redesigned frame was featured for 1967, and featured a stronger head lug forging and large triangulated top and lower tank tubes. Larger steering head bearing cups and cones, with 20 x $^1/_4$in balls, harmonised with the 650 range. The new frame head angle was changed from 65 degrees to 62 degrees, and the new steering head had provision for the Yale steering lock plunger.
  The new rear frame was fitted with welded triangular plates which bolted to the swing arm spindle, thus making a very rigid mounting for the pivot area. A side panel was fitted to the left side to tidy the area under the seat. To comply with US competition regulations, the rider's footrests were now of the folding type.

Forks A new top fork with the provision for fitting a Yale-type barrel lock was specified. The plunger of the Yale lock engaged with a hole in the steering head lug.

Petrol tank A new petrol tank with a three point fixing to suit the new frame was featured. The rear single fixing was by a shouldered bolt threaded into the frame boss.

Oil tank From H53357, the rocker feed take-off reverted to the bottom of the tank, as per pre-1966. It had been found that the top feed was causing premature wear of the valves and rockers due to intermittent lubrication.

Brakes As 1965.

Wheels As 1966.

Tyres As 1965.

Mudguards Stainless steel mudguards replaced the painted alloy ones as previously fitted.

Exhaust system Twin, high level upswept pipes, over the chaincase on the left side. The pipes terminated into small barrel-shaped silencers. Leg shields were fitted to protect the rider's leg.

1961-1974 unit construction 490cc

For 1967, the T100C was given a new frame with a stronger head lug, similar to the 650cc.

The rear frame was new for the 1967 season, with outrigger plates bolted to the pivot tube.

The Triumph Trophy Bible

Air filter As 1963.

Electrical The Lucas $5^3/_4$in headlamp shell was now chrome plated. A fully encapsulated alternator stator was specified from H53357 (20.2.1967), putting an end to stator failure caused by the coils shorting out on the laminations due to vibration.

Speedo As 1966.

Handlebars The unpopular white handlebar grips were replaced by black Italian Gran Turisimo grips.

Seat A new seat with a slightly tipped-up rear end and Triumph Quiltop all black cover was specified. The knurled chromed seat release knob was replaced by a one-piece plastic-headed seat catch plunger.

1968 Model T100C Sports Tiger

Engine/frame numbers: H58017 to H65572
Build dates: 8.9.1967 to 13.5.1968

The major change for the 1968 season was to the electrical system, when the energy transfer ignition system and direct lighting was replaced by a 12 volt standard coil-ignition system.

Engine For 1968, the cylinder head combustion chamber hemisphere was enlarged, making the cylinder head common with the T100R. Along with this modification, the inlet valve diameter was increased to $1^{17}/_{32}$in, and overall length to $3^1/_2$in. Exhaust valve diameter remained at $1^5/_{16}$in, with overall length at $3^7/_{16}$in.

Rocker boxes were thickened around the cylinder head bolt holes, to avoid distortion due to the increased power. The cylinder base nuts were changed, for accessibility, to the twelve pointed type with UNF thread.

To combat theft, the engine number pad on the left-hand crankcase had a rolled Triumph motif, onto which the model and engine number were stamped. The tachometer drive gearbox securing screw was changed to left-hand thread, to prevent slackening in use. From H63307, oil holes through the rockers were deleted so as to strengthen the rocker arms.

The Amal Monobloc carburettor was replaced by an Amal Concentric R626/8:

Bore	26mm
Mainjet	180
Throttle valve	4
Needle	622/124
Needle position	2
Needle jet	.106

Gearbox The high gear was extended into the primary chaincase. This modification required a new oil seal and cover plate, since previously only the high gear bush had extended into the primary case.

Transmission The engine sprocket drive peg was deleted, and the rotor was keyed to the crankshaft since the coil ignition system did not require such critical rotor timing as the energy transfer. The primary outer cover was fitted with a detachable circular cover which, when removed, showed a pointer and scribed lines on the rotor to aid strobe timing.

Frame The new for 1967 front frame was continued, with only a small change to the steering lock (a shelf was added to prevent the possibility of the lock peg accidentally engaging). The rear frame now incorporated

A chrome plated headlamp graced the 1968 T100C, along with a new style tail lamp housing. Stainless steel mudguards were now fitted.

1961-1974 unit construction 490cc

two brazed-in pegs on the left down tube, to locate the detachable side panel. A small triangular bracket was welded to the front of the left-hand seat tube to take a captive nut and so allow the panel knob to be attached. The new side panel, with a compartment in its lower half, now doubled as a toolbox.

Forks A new form of hydraulic damping was used on the forks. This shuttle valve system was simple and much cheaper than the earlier tube and rod. A redesigned bottom yoke now had provision for mounting the zener diode's finned heat sink. A new left-hand upper fork cover provided a housing for the Lucas ignition switch. UNF threads were introduced on the fork assemblies.

Petrol tank To overcome petrol seepage past the petrol tap threads, bonded rubber 'O' ring Stat-O-Seal washers were fitted. At H63601 (9.4.1968), the front tank mounting bolts were replaced by UNF studs and self lock nuts.

Oil tank As 1966.

Brakes As 1965.

Wheels As 1965.

Tyres As 1965.

Mudguards As 1966.

Exhaust system As 1967.

Air filter As 1963.

Speedo/tacho As 1966.

Electrical New for the T100C was the use of coil ignition. This was a 12 volt system, with twin MA 12 Lucas coils located below the petrol tank, and a separate Lucas 2CP condenser pack fitted onto the front petrol tank mounting bracket. The Lucas 6CA contact breaker assembly had separate settings for each set of points, as well as individual rotational movement for timing each cylinder. With the normal coil ignition, the auto advance range was 12 degrees.

The 12 volt Lucas PUZ5A battery was charged by a Lucas RM19 alternator, rectified by a Lucas 2DS 506 silicon rectifier. The charge was controlled by a Lucas zener diode, fitted to the 'finned egg' heat sink mounted to the front fork yoke. A new $5^{3}/_{4}$in all chrome headlamp housed a three position toggle switch controlling the lights. Two warning lights were also housed in the lamp shell, ignition warning and high beam. The Lucas S45 ignition switch was fitted to a small housing mounted in the left-hand fork top cover.

Handlebars All as 1967.

Seat The twinseat was as 1967, but the grey lower trim band was replaced by a bright chrome plastic strip. The seat hinges were changed from forgings to pressed steel, each with a welded pivot boss.

Toolbox Now incorporated in the lower half of the detachable left-hand side panel.

1969 Model T100C Trophy 500

Engine/frame numbers: H66124 to H66976
Build dates: 22.8.1968 to 5.9.1968
Engine/frame numbers: XC07583 to EC19426
Build dates: 30.12.1968 to 17.5.1969

A new prefix code came into use, from XC07583. The first letter related to the month of production, and the second letter related to the year. This year code should not be confused with calendar year, though, as it relates to the season year, which, in Triumph's case, usually meant August to August. The engine number was stamped onto a raised pad on the left crankcase half.

All the engine cover screws changed from BSF to UNC. From XC07583, most of the other threaded components changed to UNF.

A major improvement was the introduction of nitrided heat treated camshafts (still in E3134 form, though, with $^{3}/_{4}$in radius cam followers).

The crankshaft was now supported on the right-hand side by a ball journal bearing, replacing the bush. This modification required new crankcases. Oil was now fed from the timing cover directly onto the end of the crankshaft, via an oil seal situated in the timing cover.

The cylinder barrel wall thickness was increased to avoid cracking on high performance models. The connecting rod small end bushes were deleted, and the gudgeon pin now worked directly on the alloy of the rod. All filler plugs were fitted with 'O' rings, from EC17978, and two spot clearance mainbearings replaced three spot components in an endeavour to reduce mainbearing rumble.

The rotary valve breather was deleted in favour of a system breathing through the left hand mainbearing into the primary chaincase, and exiting at the rear of the chaincase via a D-section pipe attached to the rear mudguard.

Gearbox A redesigned camplate plunger and plunger spring, to give lighter loading but more positive location, was specified. A heavier gauge circlip was used to locate the mainshaft bearing. This required the use of a modified gearbox inner cover from DD47612, 14.4.1970.

Transmission The clutch/chainwheel housing had the cast-in pockets deleted, the outer diameter was now fully machined giving a better static balance. From EC18734, the clutch thrust washer tabs were deleted, and replaced by a plain ring.

Frame A new one-piece prop stand with a curved end was fitted, giving more ground clearance when in the folded position. The Girling suspension units remained, but exposed chrome springs with 100lb/in rate were fitted, with castellated spring adjusters. A new deeper rear chainguard was featured from XC07583.

The 1969 T100C tank. Note the Trophy 500 motif on the left of the petrol tank, and the new badges.

Forks The new forks introduced for the 1968 season were retained, but were fitted into the new wider top and bottom yokes. The wider centres (from $6^{1}/_{2}$in to $6^{3}/_{4}$in), allowed more mudguard/tyre clearance (this was deemed desirable on cross-country riding). From EC18711, two $^{5}/_{64}$in diameter holes, 1in from the bush shoulder and 1in apart, were added to the fork stanchions to improve the damping.

Petrol tank A new tank badge with a plain front 'beak' replaced the bird wing pattern. The new badge had the Triumph motif set within a square picture frame border. A redesigned centre styling strip with hook attachment was fitted.

Oil tank The oil tank filler cap was fitted with a dip stick.

Brakes From XC07583, the front brake was uprated, with a 7in fully floating twin leading shoe pattern. The anchor plate featured a chromed wire mesh air scoop, and the two cam levers were connected by an adjustable forked rod. The rear brake was as 1965.

Wheels The front wheel was fitted with a longer wheel spindle to compensate for the wider forks. The chrome styling cover now featured concentric ribs, replacing the earlier plain styling cover.

Tyres As 1965.

Mudguards A new front mudguard bottom stay was fitted to clear the brake cam levers. The rear mudguard was modified to accommodate the D-section breather pipe, with holes added to take the breather pipe retaining clips.

Exhaust system The two high level exhaust pipes were now linked together by a separate 'H' piece, just before entering the silencers. A new chrome plated wire leg guard now protected both the rider and pillion passenger. The silencer bodies were larger than before, with both silencer ends now finishing in line.

Air filter As 1963.

Electrical From XC07583, a switch was fitted into the front brake cable, whereby compression of the cable illuminated the stop/tail lamp. The latest offering from Lucas, in the form of the encapsulated RM21 alternator, provided power for the electrical items. Both Siba and Lucas 17 M12 ignition coils were specified, with Siba being generally used on the T100C for the USA. From XC07583, a Smiths oil pressure switch was fitted in the timing cover, electrically illuminating an indicator housed in the headlamp shell.

1961-1974 unit construction 490cc

The 'chip basket' leg protector and the 1969 method of attaching the passenger grab rail.

Speedometer As 1966.

Handlebars As 1967.

Seat As 1967.

With the introduction of the date code on the T100C, an error was made in the stamping of the code. The letter C was the correct code year for the 1969 season, but on the January-built machines, which should have been AC coded, AD was used. This error related to 1145 machines, AD07740 to AD08884, all January 1969 built machines. For year identification, therefore, only the number should be used.

1970 Model T100C Trophy 500

Engine/frame numbers: KD28652 to KD60261
Build dates: 25.9.1969 to 12.9.1970

Engine The right-hand main bearing spacer was deleted, since the new crankshaft allowed the main bearing housing to be machined to the correct dimensions.

Gearbox A gear shaving process was introduced into the production sequence, aimed at giving quieter operation and longer life. A precision pressing was now used to manufacture the camplate.

Transmission As 1969.

Frame The prop stand was fitted with an adjustable stop bolt. Whist not very important to the T100C, on the low exhaust pipe models, however, it prevented the stand crashing into the pipe.

Forks The wheel spindle end cap bolts were replaced by studs and nuts, aiding reassembly. The brazed threaded bossed on the extruded fork bottom members were replaced by welded pressings with loose square nuts.

Petrol tank As 1969.

Oil tank As 1969, except that the rear chain oiler was deleted.

Brakes The rear brake tubular torque stay was replaced by a flat strip pattern.

Wheels As 1969.

Tyres As 1965.

Mudguards The front mudguard was modified to accept the redesigned bottom stay, which now had two fixing ears thus improving safety. A new rear mudguard stay now combined with the passenger grab rail.

Exhaust system As 1969.

Air filter As 1963.

Electrical Lucas 12 volt 17M ignition coils were standardised.

Speedometer/tacho Speedo: SSM 500/02, tacho: RSM 3003/13.

Handlebars As 1967.

Seat The seat pan pressing deleted the welded threaded

The Triumph Trophy Bible

A new passenger grab rail was introduced for the 1970 season.

bosses which took the bolt-on passenger grab rail. The seat cover now featured black pierced Ambla, but retained the chrome plastic trim.

1971 Model T100C Trophy 500

Engine/frame numbers: KE00058 to GE25135
Build dates: 14.9.1970 to 6.6.1971

Engine Stronger connecting rods were introduced (they were thicker around the H-section). The rocker boxes were fitted with side plugs to assist tappet setting. Originally fitted with a copper washer, the side plugs were later fitted with 'O' rings.

The Amal Concentric carburettor bowl now had a cast-in weir, and was fitted with a removable plug for draining. A new carburettor number, 626/32, was raised by Amal replacing 626/25.

Holes replaced castellations on the push rod cover tubes.

Gearbox As 1970.

Transmission Shims were added to the specification, and fitted between the engine sprocket and the bearing to aid chain alignment.

Frame As 1970.

1961-1974 unit construction 490cc

Forks New headlamp mounting brackets were rubber mounted to the top fork covers. The left-hand headlamp bracket still housed the ignition switch.

Petrol tank As 1969.

Oil tank A increased capacity oil tank, now quoted as 5½ pints, was fitted. All the fittings remained as before.

Brakes As 1970.

Wheels As 1969, except that the quickly detachable rear wheel was discontinued as an optional extra.

Tyres As 1965.

Mudguards The front remained as 1970. The rear mudguard had a much shorter tail, however, and was drilled to accommodate the new tail lamp housing. This new tail lamp housing was fabricated from sheet steel, with the two pressings spot welded together.

Exhaust system As 1969.

Air filter As 1963.

Electrical The $5^{3}/_{4}$in chrome headlamp was fitted with three warning lights: headlamp high beam, oil pressure warning, and direction indicator. The Lucas 57SA three position toggle switch was retained.

New for this season were front and rear direction indicators. Lucas aluminium switch consoles were now fitted on the left and right of the handlebars. These new switches also provided the fulcrum for the brake and clutch levers. To match the new tin tail lamp housing, the Lucas tail lamp L679 was specified. Orange side reflectors were fitted to the rear grab rail and to small metal housings attached to the front tank mounting studs.

Speedo As 1972.

Handlebars New aluminium switch consoles, clutch and brake levers.

Direction indicators, tin tail lamp housing, and handlebar switch consoles, were the most noticeable items on the 1971 Trophy 500.

The Triumph Trophy Bible

The 1971 T100C was now fitted with direction indicators.

Seat As 1970.

The last T100C built by the Triumph Eng. Co. Ltd. was GE 25135 on 6.6.1971.

1972 Model TR5T Trophy Trail

Engine/frame numbers: GH 15001 to GH 15003
Build dates: 23.6.1972 to 23.6.1972

Built as 1973 season models.

1973 Model TR5T Trophy Trail

Engine/frame numbers: KH 16597 to GH 34399
Build dates: 7.9.1972 to 1.6.1973

A completely new model for 1973, the TR5T Trophy Trail owed very little to the previous T100C, except for the 490cc unit construction engine/gearbox unit.

The new frame closely followed the BSA Victor MX, with the oil tank integrated within the frame tubes. Conical aluminium alloy hubs were featured, as were aluminium fork yokes and bottom members.

A two gallon aluminium petrol tank, fitted with a hinged flip-up filler cap, was featured.

The TR5T was only produced for one full season, and, with a total of only 2552 manufactured, is a fairly rare machine by Triumph standards.

TR5T models were ridden in the International Six Day Trial, held in the Berkshire area of Massachusetts USA in 1973, and helped Great Britain to gain second place behind Czechoslovakia.

The winning team won with a clean sheet, whilst the British team lost only four marks. Individually, the British TR5T-mounted riders gained three gold medals and one silver.

Engine Same as 1971 T100C.

Spark plug Champion N4.

Carburettor
Type	Amal Concentric 928/21
Main jet	180
Needle jet	.106
Needle	STD 2 ring
Needle position	2
Throttle valve	3
Bore	28mm

Gearbox
Gearbox sprocket	18
Gear ratios:	
4th	6.57
3rd	8.04
2nd	11.6
1st	18.7
Engine rpm at 10mph	857 in top gear

Frame
Steering head bearings	Taper roller $^3/_4$ x $1^{25}/_{32}$in
Frame head angle	63 degrees

Rear suspension
Unit type	Girling
Length between centres	12.9in
Spring colour	Green Green
Spring free length	8.4in

Front forks
Total fork travel	$6^3/_4$in
Stanchion diameter	34mm
Stanchion length	22in

1961-1974 unit construction 490cc

The new for 1973 TR5T Trophy Trail/Adventurer.

Spring free length	19 1/8 in
Spring wire diameter	0.168in

Wheels
Rim size front	WM1 x 21
Rim size rear	WM3 x 18
Tyre size front	3.00 x 21 Dunlop Trials Universal
Tyre size rear	4.00 x 18 Dunlop Trials Universal.

Wheel bearings
Front	Ball journal 20 x 47 x 14mm
Rear	Ball journal 20 x 47 x 14mm

Brakes
Front	6in SLS, conical
Rear	7in SLS, conical

Rear wheel sprocket 53 teeth.

Rear chain 5/8 x 3/8in 110 links.

Mudguards Chrome plated steel. The front mudguard was mounted on a plate fixed to the bottom fork yoke.

Exhaust system Siamezed under the engine into a large silencer, which was shaped to fit under the gearbox and around the rear wheel. The silencer terminated near the rear wheel spindle on the right side.

Air filter A large waxed paper filter in a fibreglass box was sandwiched between the frame tubes above the gearbox.

Electrical equipment The normal 12 volt Lucas system was fitted, with a 5 1/2 in chrome headlamp. Front indicators were mounted on the handlebars, whilst the rear indicators were mounted on the rear mudguard fixing stay. Lucas 17M 12 volt coils were housed on a plate tucked up behind the gearbox. The combined horn/indicator/dip switch was originally a Yamaha component, subsequently used without the Yamaha logo.

Handlebars The wide high-rise bars were cross-braced, and solidly mounted to the top yoke.

Saddle The fibreglass based seat was only 22in long, and only suitable for one person.

Speedo/tacho Nippon Denso chrome plated instruments were fitted, with the speedo having an adjustable trip to 1/10 mile. Speedo/tacho cables were unique to these instruments.

Finish
Petrol tank	Polished alloy with Hunting Yellow, black lined side panels

131

Wheel hubs	Polished alloy, clear laquered
Brake anchor plates	Eggshell black
Fork yokes	Natural alloy
Fork sliders	Polished alloy
Mudguards	Chrome plated steel
Rest of painted parts	Gloss black

Dimensions

Wheelbase	55in
Overall length	85in
Overall width	32in
Seat height	32in
Weight (dry)	322lb
Ground clearance	7½in

Capacities

Petrol tank	2 gallons
Oil tank	4 pint, 20-50W
Telescopic forks	190cc, ATF 10-15W
Gearbox	375cc, 90 EP

For dimensions not listed read as for T100C

1974 Model TR5T Trophy Trail Adventurer

Engine/frame numbers: HJ 56408 to HJ 57336
Build dates: 5.7.1973 to 20.7.1973

Built to 1973 specification.

Finish

Petrol tank	Polished alloy, with red and gold lined panels

Appendix

Colour chart TR5, TR6, TR7

Year	Component	Description
1949	Petrol tank	Chrome plated, with Silver Sheen top and dark blue lined side panels ($1/16$in outer, $1/4$in inner lines). The badge had blue lettering on a silver background.
	Mudguards	Silver Sheen with black centre stripe with dark blue lining.
	Wheel rims	Silver Sheen painted centres with dark blue lining.
	Rest of paint	Gloss Black.
1951	Petrol tank	Painted Silver Sheen with dark blue lining, following the 1949 top and side panel shapes. Otherwise as 1949.
1952	Wheel rims	Fully painted rims in Silver Sheen, with dark blue lining. Otherwise as 1951.
1953		As 1951.
1954	Petrol tank	Chrome plated with Shell Blue Sheen top and black lined side panels. The badge had white lettering on a black background.
	Mudguards	Shell Blue Sheen with black centre stripe with white lining.
	Wheel rims	Shell Blue Sheen painted centres with black lining.
	Rest of paint	Gloss Black.
1955	Petrol tank	Shell Blue Sheen with chrome styling bands and black insets. The badge had white lettering on a black background.
	Mudguards	Shell Blue Sheen with black centre stripe with white lining.
	Wheel rims	Shell Blue Sheen painted centres with black lining.
	Rest of paint	Gloss Black.
1956	Headlamps	Plain chrome.
	Wheel rims	Plain chrome.
	Rest of paint	As 1955.
1957	Petrol tank	Crystal Silver Grey. The badge had white lettering on a black background.
	Mudguards	Crystal Silver Grey with black centre stripe and black lining.
	Front hub	Black eggshell finish - TR5 only.
	Optional finish	TR6 only.
	Petrol tank	Ivory White and Aztec Red with gold lining.
	Mudguards	Ivory White with

The Triumph Trophy Bible

	Rest of paint	Aztec Red centre stripe and gold lining. Gloss Black.			Alaskan White with black lining. The badge had black lettering on a white background.
1958		As 1957.		Mudguards	Alaskan White with Burnished Gold centre stripe and black lining. Otherwise as 1963.
	Front hub	Black eggshell finish.			
1959	Petrol tank	Ivory White and Aztec Red with gold lining. The badge had white lettering on a black background.	1966	Petrol tank	Pacific Blue and Alaskan White with gold lining. The badge had black lettering on a white background.
	Mudguards	Ivory White with Aztec Red centre stripes and gold lining.		Mudguards	Alaskan White with Pacific Blue centre stripe and gold lining. Otherwise as 1963.
	Front hub	Black eggshell finish.			
	Rest of paint	Gloss Black.			
1960		As 1959.	1967	Petrol tank	Mist Green and Alaskan White with gold lining. The badge had black lettering on a white background.
1961	Petrol tank	Ruby Red and Silver Sheen with gold lining. The badge had white lettering on a black background.			
	Mudguards	Silver Sheen with Ruby Red centre stripe and gold lining.		Mudguards	Mist Green with Alaskan White centre stripe with gold lining. Otherwise as 1963.
	Rest	As 1959.			
	Rest of paint	Gloss Black.	1968	Petrol tank	Riviera Blue and Silver Sheen with gold lining. The badge had black lettering on a white background.
1962	Petrol tank	Burgundy Red and Silver Sheen with gold lining. The badge had black lettering on a gold background.			
	Mudguards	Silver Sheen with Burgundy centre stripe and gold lining.		Mudguards	Silver Sheen with Riviera Blue centre stripe and gold lining. Otherwise as 1963.
	Front hub	Black eggshell finish.			
	Rest of paint	Gloss Black.	1969	Petrol tank	Trophy Red and Silver Sheen with gold lining. US - Trophy Red. The badge on both models had black lettering on a white background.
1963	Petrol tank	Regal Purple and Silver Sheen with gold lining. The badge had white lettering on a black background.			
	Mudguards	Silver Sheen with Regal Purple centre stripe and gold lining.		Mudguards	Trophy Red with Silver Sheen centre stripe and gold lining.
	Front hub	Silver Sheen.	TR6C		Polished stainless steel. Otherwise as 1963.
	Rest of paint	Gloss Black.	1970	Petrol tank	Spring Gold with black centre stripe and gold lining. The badge had black lettering on a white background.
1964	Petrol tank	Hi-Fi Scarlet and Silver Sheen with gold lining.			
	Mudguards	Silver Sheen with Hi-Fi Scarlet centre stripe and gold lining. Otherwise as 1963.		Mudguards	Spring Gold.
			TR6C		Polished stainless steel. Otherwise as 1963.
1965	Petrol tank	Burnished Gold and	1971	Petrol tank	Pacific Blue and Cold

Appendix

	Mudguards	White with black lining. The UK badge had black lettering on a silver transfer. The US badge had black lettering on a white background. Pacific Blue.
TR6C		Chrome plated steel.
	Wheel hubs	Silver Grey.
	Brake plates	Silver Grey.
	Tail lamp housing	Silver Grey.
	Rest of paint	Gloss Black.
1972	Petrol tank	Polychromatic Blue and Cold White with black lining. The badge had black lettering on a white background.
	Mudguards	Polychromatic Blue.
TR6C		Chrome plated steel.
	Fork sliders	Polished alloy.
	Brake plates	Black - semi-matt.
	Tail lamp housing	Black. Otherwise as 1971.
1973	Petrol tank	Astral Blue and Ice White with gold lining. The badge had black lettering on a white background.
	Mudguards	Chrome plated steel.
	Tail lamp housing	Polished alloy.
	Wheel hubs	Polished alloy.
	Upper fork covers	UK - Gloss black, US - Chrome plate. Otherwise as 1971.
1974	Petrol tank	Sea Jade Green and Ice White with gold lining. The badge had black lettering on a white background. Otherwise as 1973.
1975		
1976		
1977		All as 1974.
1978	Petrol tank	UK - Crimson Red with silver side panel and a gold inner line with a black outer. US - Crimson Red with silver scallops with gold and black lining. Both badges had black lettering on a white background.
	Mudguards	UK - Silver with Crimson Red U-shaped styling bands with gold and black lining. US - Chrome plated steel.
	Upper fork covers	Chrome plated steel.
	Wheel hubs	Silver Grey painted. Otherwise as 1973.
1979	Petrol tank	UK - Astral Blue and Silver, with black inner and gold outer lining. US - Black with Silver scallops and gold lining, or Candy Apple Red with black scallops with gold lining, or Astral Blue with silver scallops and gold lining.
	Mudguards	Chrome plated steel.
	Side panels	As main tank colour. Otherwise as 1973.
1980	Petrol tank	Silver Blue sheen with twin gold and dark blue lining.
	Side panels	Black. Otherwise as 1973.
1981	Petrol tank	UK - As 1980. US - Olympic Flame with Ivory White scallops and gold lining. The badge had chrome lettering on a black background.
	Mudguards	Polished stainless steel.
	Side panels	Black for Blue Sheen tank. Olympic Flame for US tank.
TR7T	Petrol tank	Yellow with black transfer badge.
	Mudguards	Yellow.
	Side panels	Yellow.
	Forks sliders	Black semi-matt.
TR65T		As TR7T in Bright Green.
TR65	Petrol tank	Smoked Burgundy with a single gold line. The badge had chrome lettering on a black background.
	Mudguards	Polished stainless steel.
	Side panels	Smoked Burgundy.
	Fork sliders	Black semi-matt.
	Exhaust	Black semi-matt.
	Engine side covers	Black semi-matt.
	Headlamp shell	Black semi-matt.
1982	Petrol tank	UK - Smoky Flame

135

		with single gold contour line, or Smoky Blue with a single gold contour line. US - Smoky Flame with Ivory White gull wing panels and gold lining, or Smoky Blue with Silver panels and gold lining, or Black with Candy Apple Red panels and gold lining. The badge on all models had chrome lettering on a black background.
	Mudguards	Polished stainless steel.
	Side panels	To match main tank colour.
	Fork sliders	Black semi-matt.
	Fork top covers	Black semi-matt.
1983	As 1982.	

Colour chart 500 unit

1961	Petrol tank	Kingfisher Blue and Silver Sheen with gold lining. The tank badge had white lettering on a black background.
	Mudguards	Silver Sheen with Kingfisher Blue centre stripe and gold lining.
	Front hub	Black eggshell finish.
	Rest of paint	Gloss black.
1962	Petrol tank	Burgundy Red and Silver Sheen with gold lining. The badge had black lettering on a gold background.
	Mudguards	Silver Sheen with Burgundy centre stripe and gold lining. Otherwise as 1961.
1963	Petrol tank	Regal Purple and Silver Sheen and gold lining.
	Mudguards	Silver Sheen with Purple centre stripe and gold lining. Otherwise as 1961.
1964	Petrol tank	Hi-Fi Scarlet and Silver Sheen with gold lining. The badge had white lettering on a black background.
	Mudguards	Silver Sheen with Scarlet centre stripe and gold lining.
	Front hub	Silver Sheen.
	Rest of paint	Gloss Black.
1965	Petrol tank	Alaskan White and Sherbourne Green and gold lining. The badge had black lettering on a white background.
	Mudguards	Alaskan White with Sherbourne Green centre stripe and gold lining. Otherwise as 1964.
1966		As 1965 for US East Coast. As 1965 for US West Coast, but with polished aluminium mudguards.
	Tail lamp housing	Polished alloy.
1967	Petrol tank	Pacific Blue and Alaskan White with gold lining. The badge had black lettering on a white background.
	Mudguards	Polished stainless steel.
	Tail lamp housing	Polished alloy.
	Headlamp	Chrome plated.
	Rest of paint	Gloss Black.
1968	Petrol tank	Aquamarine. Otherwise as 1967.
1969	Petrol tank	Lincoln Green. Otherwise as 1967.
1970	Petrol tank	Jacaranda Purple with silver central stripe and gold lining. Otherwise as 1967.
1973	Petrol tank	Polished aluminium with Hunting Yellow side panels and black lining. The TR5T tank transfer had black lettering on silver.
	Mudguards	Chrome plated.
	Wheel hubs	Silver Grey sheen.
	Brake plates	Silver Grey sheen.
	Fork sliders	Polished alloy.
	Tail lamp housing	Polished alloy.
	Rest of paint	Gloss Black.
1974	Petrol tank	Hi-Fi Vermillion side panels with gold lining.
	Wheel hubs	Polished alloy.
	Brake plates	Semi-matt black.
	Rear guard stay	Chrome plated. Otherwise as 1973.

Appendix

Model year build totals

YEAR	1949	1950	1951	1952	1953	1954	1955	1956	1957	1958	1959	1960	1961	1962	1963	1964	1965	1966
TR5	457	305	783	255	398	227	872	215	121	860	101							
TR5R								112	17	49								
TR6							1	1678	1691	1691	1254	1221					1220	637
TR6B												402						
TR6C													310			192		543
TR6R													1108			963		1529
TR6SR																478	922	1631
TR6SS														1266	1685	447	182	83
TR6SC																60	346	260
TR5AR													470					
TR5AC													635					
T100C														281	71	758	1200	2709

YEAR	1967	1968	1969	1970	1971	1972	1973	1974	1975	1976	1977	1978	1979	1980	1981	1982	1983
TR6	262	357	377	682													
TR6C	2042	1573	2772	1880	3056	1150											
TR6CV						2											
TR6R	4706	2673	4900	6246	7527	3607											
TR6P	570	977	852	1323	154	752	25										
TR6RV					1	2047	122										
TR7RV							6234	25	5	690	1348	406	597	292	68	28	36
TR7RVS															48	2	149
TR7P							79				8						
TR7T																153	10
TR27													16	10			
TR65																243	168
TR65T																	3
TR7AV																5	
T100C	2841	3593	3195	4220	2250												
TR5T							2155	929									

Works registered Trophy models

Reg no	Model	Year	Use	Comment
JAC 564	TR5	1949	ISDT	
JAC 565	TR5	1949	ISDT	
JAC 566	TR5	1949	ISDT	
HUE 258	TR5	1950	One day trials	
HUE 259	TR5	1950	One day trials	
HUE 260	TR5	1950	One day trials	
KAC 677	TR5	1950	ISDT	
KAC 678	TR5	1950	ISDT	
KAC 679	TR5	1950	ISDT	
LNX 341	TR5	1951	ISDT	Later changed to one day trials specification
LNX 351	TR5	1951	ISDT	Later changed to one day trials specification
LNX 361	TR5	1951	ISDT	650cc 6T engine fitted
MNX 62	TR5	1952	ISDT	
MNX 64	TR5	1952	ISDT	650cc 6T engine fitted
NAC 453	TR5	1953	One day trials	Originally rigid frame - rebuilt with s/arm frame
NUE813	TR5	1953	ISDT	
NUE 814	TR5	1953	ISDT	Originally rigid frame - rebuilt with s/arm frame
NUE 815	TR5	1953	ISDT	
NWD 198	TR5	1953	ISDT	650cc 6T engine fitted
NWD 199	TR5	1953	ISDT	650cc 6T engine fitted
PNX 388	TR5	1954	ISDT	650cc 6T engine fitted

The Triumph Trophy Bible

Reg no	Model	Year	Use	Comment
PNX 660	TR5	1954	ISDT	
PNX 661	TR5	1954	ISDT	Later changed to one day trials specification
PUE 727	TR5	1954	ISDT	
PUE 728	TR5	1954	ISDT	
SAC 980	TR5	1955	ISDT	
SAC 981	TR5	1955	ISDT	
SAC 982	TR5	1955	ISDT	
UAC 373	TR5	1956	ISDT	
UAC 374	TR5	1956	ISDT	
UAC 375	TR6	1956	ISDT	
RWD 318	TR5	1957	One day trials	
YNX 962	TR6	1958	ISDT	
YNX 963	TR6	1958	ISDT	
YWD 210	TR6	1958	Test mileage Motorcycle	
RWD 853	TR6	1958	ISDT	
608 BWD	TR6	1960	Test mileage Motorcycle	
565 AAC	TR5AC	1961	Test mileageMotorcycle	
777 BWD	TR6	1961	ISDT	
119 CAC	TR5AC	1961	ISDT	
120 CAC	TR5AC	1961	ISDT	
230 CAC	TR5AC	1961	ISDT	
105 CWD	T100C	1962	ISDT	Fitted with 350cc engine
106 CWD	T100C	1962	ISDT	
895 BUE	TR6	1962	ISDT	Built for Bud Ekins
929 FNX	TR6	1963	ISDT	
678 CUE	T100C	1963	ISDT	
562 FNX	T100C	1963	One day trials	Fitted with 350cc engine
117 LAC	TR6	1964	ISDT	
BNX 822B	TR6	1964	ISDT	Built for Steve McQueen
HUE 252D	T100C	1965	ISDT	Fitted with 350cc engine
HUE 253D	T100C	1965	ISDT	
HUE 254D	T100C	1965	ISDT	Fitted with 350cc engine
HUE 255D	T100C	1965	ISDT	Enlarged 504cc engine
HUE 256D	T100C	1965	ISDT	Enlarged 504cc engine
KUE 4D	TR6	1967	Press test motorcycle	
MNX 13E	T100C	1967	Press test motorcycle	
VWD 582H	TR6	1970	Press test motorcycle	
AWD 252J	T100C	1071	Press test motorcycle	
JWD 290L	TR5T	1972	Test mileage motorcycle	
JWD 291 L	TR5T	1972	Test mileage motorcycle	
KUE 471 L	TR7RV	1973	Test mileage motorcycle	

This list does not comprise all the works registered trophy motorcycles as the records are incomplete

Notable registration numbers associated with the Trophy model

Reg. number	Model	Year	Use	Comment
ENX 674	3T	1946	One day trials	The first trials twin for Triumph
EUE 319	3T	1946	One day trials	
EUE 347	3T	1946	One day trials	
GUE 223	3TR	1946	Press test motorcycle	Also one day trials machine
FDG 647	3T	1947	One day trials	
FUE 492	3T/5T	1947	Scottish six days trials	
HHP 90	5T	1948	ISDT	Speed Twin trials machines. All three finished with a gold medal and the manufacturers team award.
HHP 91	5T	1948	ISDT	
HHP 92	5T	1948	ISDT	

Appendix

Trophy show models

Engine/frame numbers of machines built for various shows throughout the world.

Model	Number	Built	Venue
TR5	TC 1 1002T 106002	14.01.1949	Brussels
TR5	11 18N	12.10.1949	Earls Court
TR5	1438N	27.09.1950	Paris
TR5	14747N	04.10.1950	Works showroom
TR5	33866	06.11.1952	Earls Court
TR5	33867	06.11.1952	Earls Court
TR5	45595	07.11.1953	Earls Court
TR5	58995	13.10.1954	Earls Court
TR5	58996	13.10.1954	Earls Court
TR5	61280	08.12.1954	Brussels
TR6	71634	13.09.1955	Earls Court
TR5	71635	13.09.1955	Earls Court
TR5	72123	27.09.1955	Paris
TR6	2072	08.10.1956	Earls Court
TR5	2074	08.10.1956	Earls Court
TR6	11861	21.10.1957	Milan
TR6	11862	21.10.1957	Milan
TR5R	12359	04.11.1957	Milan
TR5	13266	09.12.1957	Works showroom
TR5R	14807	04.02.1958	To Tokyo Show, Japan
TR6	020883	08.11.1958	Earls Court
TR6	D3171	08.02.1960	Works showroom
TR5AC	H18635	01.09.1960	Earls Court
TR5AR	H18636	01.09A960	Earls Court
TR6C	D7722	05.11.1960	Earls Court
TR6C	D8329	12.11.1960	Paris
TR6	DU102	29.09.1962	Earls Court & Paris
TR6S/S	DU561	10.12.1962	Works showroom
TR6S/S	DU7327	15.11.1963	Works showroom
TR6	DU14782	10.09.1964	Earls Court
TR6S/S	DU15357	13.10.1964	Earls Court
TR6S/S	DU15358	13.10.1964	Earls Court
TR6SR	DU25275	12.08.1965	Earls Court
T100C	H49834	29.08.1966	Duarte-USA
T100C	H51041	15.10.1966	Earls Court
TR6R	DU46300	29.09.1966	Earls Court
TR6R	DU46302	29.09.1966	Earls Court
TR6P	DU46303	29.09.1966	Earls Court
TR6R	DU46663	29.09.1966	Paris
TR6R	DU46664	29.09.1966	Paris
TR6R	DU46665	29.09.1966	Paris
TR6R	DU46666	29.09.1966	Paris
TR6R	DU46667	29.09.1966	Paris
TR6R	DU46668	29.09.1966	Paris
TR6R	DU46884	05.10.1966	Earls Court
TR6R	DU46885	05.10.1966	Earls Court
TR6R	HD023795	09.07.1969	Earls Court
TR6	HD023796	09.07.1969	Earls Court
TR6C	HD023797	09.07.1969	Earls Court
TR6	HD023799	09.07.1969	Earls Court
TR6C	HD024347	15.07.1969	Earls Court
TR6R	HD024348	15.07.1969	Earls Court
TR6C	HD024349	15.07.1969	Earls Court
TR6R	HD024350	15.07.1969	Earls Court
TR6C	HD024351	15.07.1969	Earls Court
TR6R	HD024352	15.07.1969	Earls Court

The Triumph Trophy Bible

Model	Number	Built	Venue
TR6R	HG030872	16.07.1971	Earls Court
TR6R	HG030873	16.07.1971	Earls Court
TR6C	HG030874	16.07.1971	Earls Court
TR6C	HG030875	16.07.1971	Earls Court
TR6RV	HG030876	16.07.1971	Earls Court
TR6RV	HG030877	16.07.1971	Earls Court
TR6CV	HG03078	16.07.1971	Earls Court
TR6CV	HG03079	16.07.1971	Earls Court
TR7RV	JB27513	14.08.1980	Earls Court
TR65	BEA33003	05.02.1982	NEC Birmingham
TR65	BEA33004	05.02.1982	NEC Birmingham
TR65T	BEA33009	05.02.1982	NEC Birmingham

Trophy carburettor specification

Model	Year	Carburettor type	Amal no.	Main jet	Needle jet	Needle	Needle position	Throttle valve	Pilot jet	Nominal bore size	Comment
TR5	1949-50	276-6	276DK/IA	150	0.107	6	3	3.5		15/16in	
TR5	1951-54	276-6	276FF/IAT	150	0.107	6	3	3.5		1in	
TR5	1955	276-6	276DK/IA	150	0.107	6	3	3.5		1in	fitted with large TT type float chamber
TR5	1955-58	Monobloc	376/35	220	0.1065	C	3	3.5	25	15/16in	
TR5R	1957	276-6	276/AO/AN	200	0.109	6	2	4		1in	twin type 6 with remote float chamber Amal 14/538
TR5R	1957	Monobloc	376	210	0.106	C	3	3.5	25	1in	twin monobloc on splayed port cylinder head
TR5AC	1961	Monobloc	376/23	190	0.106	C	3	3.5	25	1in	
T100C	1962-67	Monobloc	376/23	190	0.106	C	3	3.5	25	1in	
T100C	1968-69	Concentric	R626/8	180	0.106	2 ring	2	4		26mm	
T100C	1970-72	Concentric	R626/25	170	0.106	2 ring	2	4		26mm	cast in weir and removable plug in float chamber
TR6	1956	289	289	200	0.107	29	3	4		1 1/16in	fittted with large TT type float chamber
TR6	1957-63	Monobloc	376/40	250	0.106	C	3	3.5	25	1 1/16in	fitted from engine number 71624
TR6	1964-66	Monobloc	389/97	310	0.106	D	1	3.5	25	1 1/8in	
TR6	1967-69	Concentric	R930/23	230	0.106	2 ring	2	3.5		30mm	
TR6	1970-72	Concentric	R930/60	230	0.106	2 ring	2	3.5		30mm	cast in weir and removable plug-in float chamber from AD 39329
TR7	1973-82	Concentric	R930/89	280	0.106	2 ring	2	3.5		30mm	
TR7T	1982-83	Concentric	R930/108	240	0.106	2 ring	1	3		30mm	
TR65	1982-83	Concentric	R9301108	240	0.106	2 ring	1	3		30mm	
TR5T	1973-74	Concentric	R928/21	180	0.106	2 ring	2	3		28mm	
TR5R	1954-56	Amal GP	10 GP	220	0.107	STD				1in	c/bored 1.0635/1.06345 dia x 13/64in deep to fit non-splayed cylinder head. Remote float bowl Amal 302. Air slide blanking plug fitted
TR5R	1957-58	Amal GP	15 GP	250	0.107	STD	3	6		1in	

Also from Veloce –

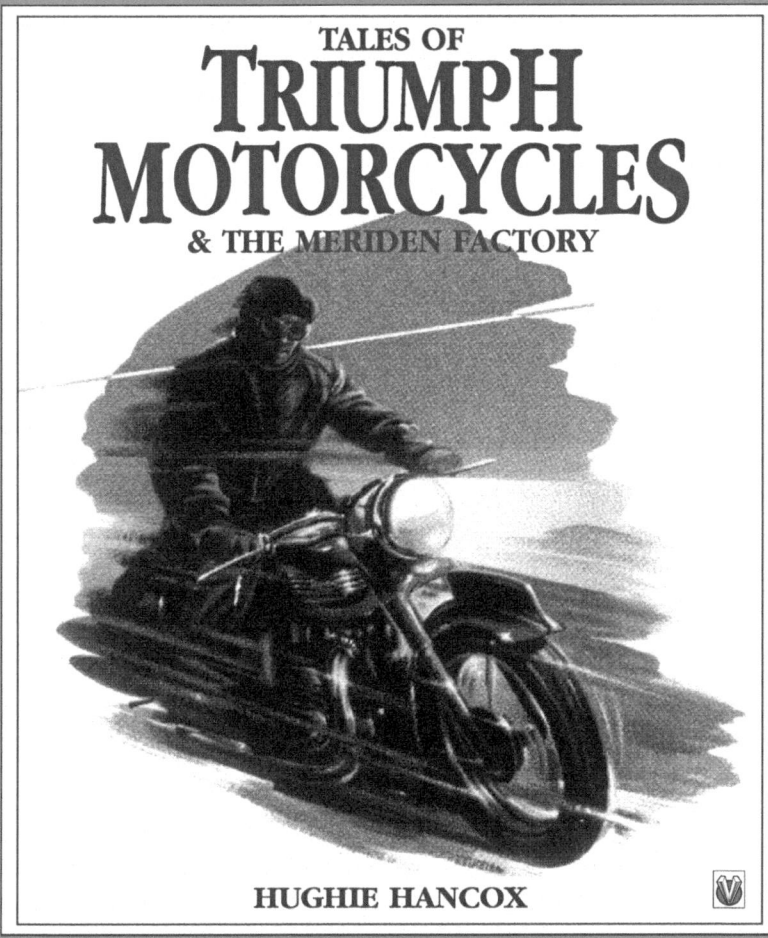

Hughie Hancox worked at Triumph from 1954 until its closure in 1974. Here's the story of his life in the famous Meriden factory; of many adventures with Triumph motorcycles & Triumph people. Records the fascinating history of a great marque.

Paperback • 25x20.7cm • £24.99 UK/$39.95 USA • 144 pages
ISBN: 978-1-901295-67-2

Having this book in your pocket is just like having a real marque expert by your side. Benefit from the author's years of Triumph ownership, learn how to spot a bad bike quickly, and how to assess a promising bike like a professional. Get the right bike at the right price!

Paperback • 19.5x13.9cm • £12.99 UK/$19.95 USA • 64 pages
• 102 colour pictures
ISBN: 978-1-845847-55-5

For info on any Veloce book, call +44 (0)1305 260068, email info@veloce.co.uk, or visit us on the web at www.veloce.co.uk
• Prices subject to change • P&P extra

Index

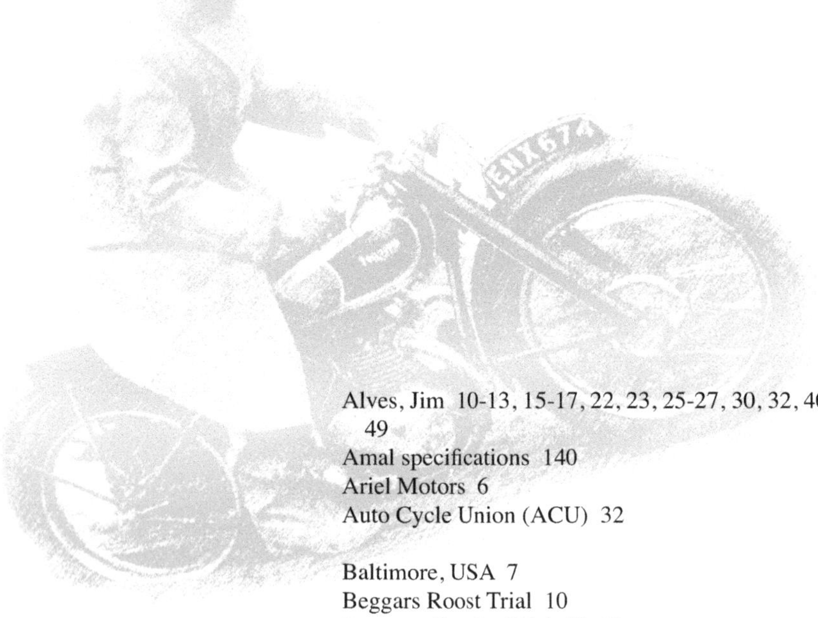

Alves, Jim 10-13, 15-17, 22, 23, 25-27, 30, 32, 40, 49
Amal specifications 140
Ariel Motors 6
Auto Cycle Union (ACU) 32

Baltimore, USA 7
Beggars Roost Trial 10
Bemrose Trophy Trial 10, 13
Bettmann, Siegfried 6
Birmingham Small Arms (BSA) 7, 8, 26, 28, 32, 33, 37, 120
BTH magneto – last fitted 50

Catalina Grand Prix 63
Colmore Cup Trial 17
Colour charts 133-136
Cotswold Cups Trial 10, 12, 13
Coventry (blitz) 7, 10
Cox, Arvin 20, 51
CZ Motorcycles 38

Davies, Ivor 20
Delta cylinder head 35
Department of Trade and Industry (DTI) 8
Duarte 37

Ekins, Bud 19-21, 49, 63, 71, 138
Ekins, Dave 20
Eustace, Brian 8

Farley, Gordon 36
FIM medals 23

Garmisch Parten-Kirchen 19

Gaymer, Albert 10, 11, 15, 16, 22, 24, 26
Generator unit 12, 14, 39
Giles, John 19, 20, 34, 36, 49, 118
Girling Ltd 50

Hammond, Peter 49
Harley Davidson 6
Heanes, Ken 33, 36
Hitchcock, Jock 26
Hopwood, Bert 7, 8
Hybrid (Triumph/BSA) 32, 33, 37

Indian Motorcycle Co 6
International Six Days Trial
  1939 13, 26
  1947 26
  1948 13, 15, 19, 22-24, 26, 40
  1949 16, 19, 23-25, 28
  1950 19, 23, 24, 26, 28
  1951 19, 23, 24, 28
  1952 26, 28-30
  1953 27
  1954 31, 32, 49
  1956 34
  1958 35
  1961 114
  1964 19
  1965 28, 33, 36
  1966 28, 78
  1967 33
  1973 36-38, 130

Jack Pine Enduro 24, 63
Jawa Motorcycles 15
Jefferies, Alan 10, 11, 15, 22, 26

Jofeh, Lionel 7, 8
Johnson Motors Inc 6
Johnson, Bill 6
Jomo 7, 25, 76, 119

Licence to acquire Triumph 6
Lloyds Bank Official Receiver 6
Lucas Energy Transfer ignition 78, 114
Lucas magneto 50, 69

Magano, Doug 20
Magnetic speedometer 73, 81, 119
Magnetic tachometer 73, 81, 119
Manns, Bob 16, 25
Manufacturers Team Awards 15, 16, 19, 22, 23, 26, 28, 33, 36
Marvin, Lee 20
Massachusetts, USA 36
McCormack, Dennis 7
Meriden Factory 7, 8
Miller, Sammy 36
Minerva 6
Mitcham Vase Trial 10
Mitchell Trial 13
Mojave Desert 20
Motorcycle Shows 19, 139

National Transport Museum 10
Needham, Mike 7
Nelson, John 20, 116
Norton Villiers 8

Page, Val 6
Pasadena 6
Peplow, Roy 36, 114
Poore, Dennis 8
Postel, Bill 20, 51
Production quantities 137

Raleigh Cycles, 6
Ratcliffe, Artie 56
Robertson, GF 13

San Remo 15, 26
Sanders, Allan 26
Sangster, Jack 6, 7
Sayer, Ray 36
Shawcross, Lord 8
Shulte, Mauritz 6
Slickshift gearbox 21
Spring wheel 7, 20
Standard Motor Company 6
Sturgeon, Harry 7
Swedish Army 56

The Great Escape 49
Tricor 7, 22, 25, 119
Triumph Corporation 7
Triumph Engineering Company Limited 6, 7, 8
Triumph Motorcycles:
  3HP (363cc) 6
  3HW 7
  3SW 7
  3T 10-13, 15
  3TR 12, 14
  3TWD 9, 10
  5SW 7
  5T 10, 13, 15, 18, 22, 26, 40
  600cc Twin 6
  633cc Twin 6
  Model H 6
  T100 10, 13, 18, 26
  T100C 25, 121-130
  T100SC 116, 117, 119-121
  T50WD 120
  T70-T80 10
  TR5 15-21, 23-26, 28, 29, 31, 33, 35, 39, 40, 44-49, 51-54, 56, 58
  TR5 650cc 26, 27, 30, 32
  TR5AC 23, 25, 107, 110-114
  TR5AR 23, 25, 107, 110, 112
  TR5R 51, 53-55, 60, 62
  TR5T 36-38, 130-132
  TR6 19-21, 25, 34, 51, 53-61, 63, 70, 71, 73-75, 78, 79, 82, 86, 87, 90, 91, 95-98
  TR65 104, 106
  TR6P 79, 80, 82, 86, 87, 90, 95, 97
  TR6R 63, 70, 72, 74, 79, 81-83, 86, 87, 89, 90, 93
  TR6RV 90, 95, 97
  TR6SC 19, 21, 63-65, 68, 72, 74, 77, 79, 82, 84, 86-88, 90, 92, 95, 97
  TR6SR 21, 72-74, 79
  TR6SS 69, 71-74
  TR7AV 104
  TR7P 97
  TR7RV 97, 99-104, 106
  TR7RVS 104-106
  TR7T 104, 106
Trophy 15
Trophybird 20
Trusty Triumph 6
Turner, Edward 6, 7
Turner, Eric 7

Umberslade Hall 7, 8

Wickes, Jack 20
World Speed Record 36
WWII 6, 7, 10

Also from Veloce –

Having this book in your pocket is just like having a real marque expert by your side. Benefit from the author's years of real ownership experience, learn how to spot a bad Bonneville quickly, and how to assess a promising one like a professional. Get the right bike at the right price!

Paperback • £12.99 UK/$19.95 USA • 64 pages • 100 colour photos
ISBN: 978-1-845841-34-8

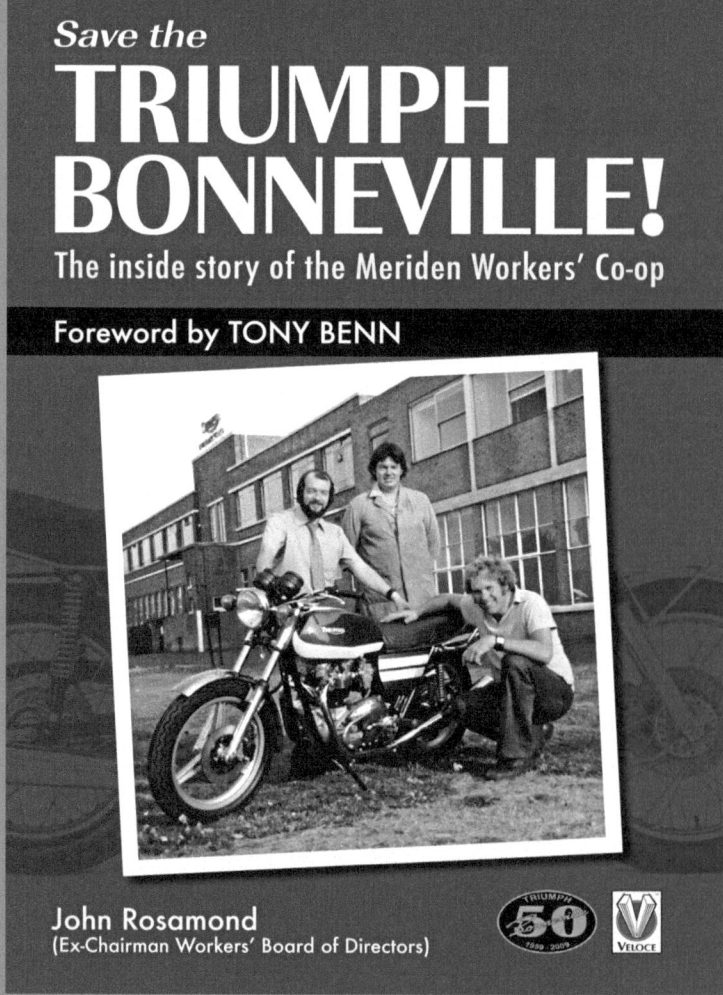

Written by the ex-Chairman of the famous Workers' Co-op, this is the real story of the last bastion of British motorcycle production following the collapse of the industry. It's also the tale of a workforce's refusal to let the Triumph Bonneville die ...

Hardback • £12.49 UK/$24.95 USA • 448 pages • 116 photos
ISBN: 978-1-845842-65-9

For info on any Veloce book, call +44 (0)1305 260068, email info@veloce.co.uk, or visit us on the web at www.veloce.co.uk
• Prices subject to change • P&P extra